THE JOY OF THE LORD IS OUR STRENGTH

EMBRACED BY GOD'S AMAZING GRACE

Jane Ann Derr

WESTBOW
PRESS®
A DIVISION OF THOMAS NELSON
& ZONDERVAN

WestBow Press books may be ordered through booksellers or by contacting:

WestBow Press
A Division of Thomas Nelson & Zondervan
1663 Liberty Drive
Bloomington, IN 47403
www.westbowpress.com
1 (866) 928-1240

ISBN: 978-1-9736-7699-7 (sc)
ISBN: 978-1-9736-7700-0 (hc)
ISBN: 978-1-9736-7698-0 (e)

Library of Congress Control Number: 2019915756

Print information available on the last page.

WestBow Press rev. date: 10/29/2019

What people are saying about Jane Ann Derr's Books

God's House! Beautiful! Let's Go!

"In God's House! Beautiful! Let's Go! Jane Ann Derr has told us more than we have a right to ask. She has let us into the world of her marriage, her family, her work, her loss, her fears, and her happiness. She has let us into her faith in God and her devotion to Jesus Christ. She has let us into her husband's illness and death, and into her grief and resolve of her life as the one who survived. But her real interest is what she has seen of the goodness and mercy of God."

Stephen Broyles
Author of *The Wind that Destroys and Heals*

"I have known Jane Ann and Harold Derr for many years . Jane Ann's faith and prayer-life stand out as she relates Harold's suffering and death. I highly recommend this book, especially for those who are called upon to pass through this valley of shadows."

Neil R. Lightfoot
Distinguished Professor Emeritus, Abilene Christian
University; author of *How We Got the Bible. Third edition
Revised and Expanded* and *Everyone's Guide to Hebrews.*

"For Harold and Jane Ann, the journey has been exceedingly fruitful. I predict that as you read this book, you will cry, you will laugh, and you will be encouraged. At least, that's what happened when I read it."

Gary Chapman
Author of *The Five Love Languages and Love as a Way of Life*

"The title of this book is God's gift to those of us who need just a peek through the curtain. Although Christians are to live by faith and not by sight, Harold Derr's description of his final vision is compelling evidence of the land that God's people have talked and sung about for so long."

Charlie Walton
Author of *When There Are No Words*

"I highly recommend Jane Ann Derr's book for anyone who has lost a love one. The theme of the book is to point us to an eternal life with Jesus and she has done that in a masterful way."

Grace J. Farrar, Widow of Dr. Henry C. Farrar
Author of *Stand By, and See What The Lord Will Accomplish*
The Story of One Family Serving the Lord in Nigeria 1964 – 1967

PRAISE FOR THE JOY OF THE LORD IS OUR STRENGTH

"Jane Derr's thoughts flow from a loving heart, a Biblically grounded mind, a deep humility, and a truly disciplined life. Jane is exceptional in all matters pertaining to faith, Godliness, and a desire to encourage. Jane writes with a firm confidence in God gained by successfully passing through life's crucibles. However difficult the experience, Jane writes with the profound joy of the Lord as her strength."

Dr. Allen D. Ferry, D Min.
Reflections of Grace; Christlike Men & Women Who Influenced My Life
Author & Friend

"Through story and song Jane Ann Derr illustrates how God again and again turns mourning into joy. In deeply personal ways, she reflects on human struggle and victory within the context of God's never-failing love and she invites us to go do the same. Both those confident in their faith and those who doubt will find encouragement here."

Martha Farrar Highfield Phd RN is Professor Emeritus of Nursing at California State University/Northridge, serves on the Board of International Health Care Foundation, volunteers in Nigeria and Haiti, and is author of a forthcoming book on Church of Christ missionary nurses.

"The Joy of the Lord is Our Strength takes readers on a journey into faith riveting stories of perseverance and provides inspiration to Christ followers. This book is awe-inspiring and absolutely a refreshing testament of Harold's and Jane Ann's faith, commitment and dedication of service to the Kingdom through several decades."

Washington J. Johnson
Retired Army Officer

"Thank you for writing yet another book instilling the importance of faith! You are a special woman with special talents. You and your family have inspired me deeply as well as my family. Your perseverance and commitment to so many people continue to be miraculous and God's calling. I continue to wish you and your family success! You truly are a special blessing! Thank you for sharing your interesting stories and providing positive encouragement to so many people with your knowledge and beautiful spirit.!"

Paula Campbell
Delta Flight Attendant, Owner of POliviaDesigns

"I have completed the reading of the manuscript you shared. Thank you for sharing with me, so I could once again have the gift of your wisdom. For those who know you and your family, or your life journey, it's a review of shared history, experience, and blessing. For those who never knew you, it's a testimony of the guidance through your life of our Heavenly Father. Your book is uplifting and encouraging, meant to be studied slowly to allow for meditation and absorption. I praise your including of so much Scripture."

Dianne Summers
Mother, Grandmother, Elementary Teacher (retired), Bible
Class teacher, Caregiver, Grief Ministry, Crafter

In *The Joy of the Lord Is Our Strength* Jane Ann Derr's candid writing of her own struggles through pain, disappointment, and even emotional collapse lead us to desire the same "life preserver" that was her salvation. Her strong relationship with God, developed over many years of Bible study, prayer, and soul-stretching service have led her to a place of joyful confidence. Very thoughtfully, she has left a "roadmap" for us, a book with many helps for our own spiritual journeys. I think I am a better person for having read this book, and I think you would be, too.

Patti Mattox Bryant, author

Truly, Jane Ann captures so much in her life's journey experiences of what it means that the joy of the Lord is her strength. She knows it and lives it. As a mentor, dear friend, and sister-in-Christ, we have shared with each other many joy-of-the-Lord-strengthening insights and praises until the early hours of the morning. Those times built me up and strengthened me in the Lord, and I cherish them. I recommend heartily her latest book, The Joy of The Lord is Our Strength – it will not only bless you, but bless you with the Lord's joy and strength.

Latrelle Elliott,
Bible teacher, Shelter Ministry
September 2019

Dedication

John Albert Derr

In Loving Memory

John Albert Derr

December 7, 1958 – August 21, 2016

Gracious Servant

Acknowledgements

To God: The Father, the Son and the Holy Spirit.

To my precious husband, Harold, for experiencing life with me on our fifty-five-year-journey as a team. Thank you, God, for sending him my way. You knew he was the perfect one for me.

To all my five precious children, my beloved friends, who have each helped me in their own unique ways.

To Deborah, who labored endlessly over many hours on the edits, and her husband, Kevin who was always available and willing to help with all my house maintenance needs as well as listening and encouraging me. I could never have completed this without both of you.

To Diana, who traveled from Hawaii to North Carolina to spend three weeks with me, visiting, encouraging, and helping with my technical needs. your visit was a breath of fresh air and helped immensely. Thank you.

To Janice who traveled from Colorado to North Carolina many times to organize, computerize and summarize my edits, and to Tim, her husband who wisely helped with many editorial issues. you are both a great treasure to me.

To Cathy who made many trips to visit me from Tennessee along with her husband Mark. Thank you both so very much. You helped me in many weak areas of my life. Your valuable time, and wise advise was much appreciated, as well as the equipment to help my fading eyesight and

Cathy's last trip to make sure i was able to complete this book. Thank you both.

To John, my precious son, the gracious servant, who was always ready to help me. Thank you, God, for allowing me to have him for fifty-seven years. I will always miss him until we meet again in Heaven with Harold and our beautiful savior Jesus Christ.

To all my precious grandchildren and great-grandchildren. You all amaze me! Fifteen grands and nineteen great-grands! Thank you, God!

To my parents, Loran and Luetta Critchlow, my brother Jack, and my aunt Ruby. Your love, caring, and sacrifice has forever impacted my perception of love, mercy, grace, patience and long-suffering. Thank you, God for the great gift of my parents and family.

To Tonie and Susie Derr, my precious in-laws. You loved me as the daughter you had always wanted. Thank you God for this great gift.

To all the many saints who God brought along side of us to show us what it means to be a Christian. You have personally encouraged me often after the passing of Harold and of John. Thank you, God for this great blessing.

To all the saints in many churches in many different States who have prayed for me, encouraged me, and read my manuscript, I thank God, for sending you to me to teach me God's wisdom.

To Pastor Rob Decker at Triad Baptist Church: I thank God for allowing me the five-year opportunity to listen weekly to your Bible-based, expository sermons, elegantly delivered with clarity and simplicity. Your prayers and other acts of kindness helped me complete this book. With deep humility and gratitude, I thank you for reading the entire manuscript and mentioning The Joy of the Lord is our Strength in a sermon and using the empty picture frame as an illustration. Thank you.

To all of my great health care providers especially Dr. Charles P. Richards at Piedmont Retina Specialists in Winston-Salem, North Carolina and all of the people at the North Carolina State Services for the Blind. You all were so kind in every way. I thank God for sending all of these people to help me.

To Dr. Allen Ferry for his part in patiently editing this book. In my discouragement, you taught me the gift of laughter. Thank you, God for sending him my way.

To my gracious, kind, patient, loving neighbor, rumiana, who spent many hours teaching me new computer skills. thank you God for my wonderful neighbor.

To all the people at West Bow Press, a division of Thomas Nelson and Zondervan, you have patiently waited for this book to give birth. I appreciate everyone who has helped. Thank you God for choosing them to be my publisher.

To all the readers, I appreciate the time you are investing in reading this book. I pray you will be encouraged to see how God took my blunders and turned them into blessings. Then you will know, if he did that for me, He will also do it for you. God is faithful.

Contents

What people are saying about Jane Ann Derr's Books vii

Dedication xi

Acknowledgements... xiii

Preface xix

Introduction - The Big Picture.. xxiii

Psalm 139 xxv

PART ONE
GOD'S OMNISCIENCE

Chapter 1   From Chaos to Calm —Psalm 139:1 1
             Reflections.. 10
Chapter 2   The Invisible Hand of God — Psalm 139:2 11
             The Deserted Graveyard.................................... 12
             Reflections...19
Chapter 3   Surprised by a Sudden Storm —Psalm 139:3................ 20
             Reflections.. 31
Chapter 4   The Dawn of a New Day —Psalm 139:4-6 32
             A Tribute To Susie Derr 34
             The Anchor Of The Soul 35
             God's Way 37
             Reflections.. 42

PART TWO
GOD'S OMNIPRESENCE

Chapter 5   The Mercy of God —Psalm 139:7-12 45
             In the Valley of Decision 49
             Reflections.. 52

PART THREE
GOD'S OMNIPOTENCE

Chapter 6   The Eternal God Formed Me —Psalm 139:13-16 55
             The Way of Peace 70
             Reflections 71
Chapter 7   Response To God's Greatness & Grace —Psalm
             139:17-18 72
             Reflections 109

PART FOUR
GOD'S HOLINESS

Chapter 8   Mysteries and Secrets —Psalm 139:19-22 113
             Reflections 129
Chapter 9   My Breath-Taking Experience —Psalm 139: 23-24 131
             Embraced by God's Amazing Grace 148
             Reflections 149

PART FIVE
HOW TO BEGIN YOUR JOURNEY WITH JOY

Notes 155
Resources for Further Study 163
Appendix 1 169
Appendix 2 179

Preface
THE JOY OF THE LORD IS OUR STRENGTH

In 2011 I started writing this book. I lived alone in the middle of the woods. My husband had struggled furiously to restore a forsaken rundown house into a home. After many years, he succeeded in transforming it into a beautiful special retreat. We had looked forward to this after fifty-five years of fast-paced challenges.

As we worked together, we overcame unbelievable obstacles while trying to acquaint people to Our Beautiful Savior, Jesus Christ. God gave us the opportunity to testify the Good News to our five children, to people in the jungles of Ghana, West Africa, to people in the Pine Barrens of South Jersey, to people in the outskirts of Death Valley, California, to people in the back hills of middle Kentucky, to people in the historic quaint beauty of Winston-Salem, North Carolina, and in the foothills of Georgia's Blue Ridge Mountains which is part of the ancient Appalachian chain.

Shortly after our restored special retreat was completed, Harold, my husband, developed cancer, went into hospice care in our home and died in the sunroom where I had been writing.

After Harold's death, I developed an unquenchable desire to ask why. In my reflective moments, I was drawn to search deeply into the subject of prayer. The pages in this book will tell what happened as I muddled through my lonely journey and craved solitude.

In my journey through grief, I have written a book about our family's missionary work in Africa. That book has been published as *Trailblazing with God: Learning to Walk on the Water* (Longwood, Florida: Xulon Press, 2008).

I have also written a book about our specific journey with grief. That book has been published as *God's House! Beautiful! Let's Go!* (Longwood, Florida: Xulon Press, 2011).

After my books were published, I still had a restless spirit. My daughter Deborah suggested I write a book on prayer. Harold would always say with a twinkle in his eye, "Be careful what you pray for and always fasten your seatbelt. God will always answer your prayer, but not the way you expected!"

In an atmosphere of choosing to remove the noise of the world, I turned off the television and social media. I read and re-read the Bible in many different translations. I read many books by various Bible scholars. I listened to many DVD courses taught by learned seminary professors. I wanted to know! I wanted to see the big picture! I wanted to connect the concepts of the Old Testament into the concepts of the New Testament and to see how God's words effected the hearts of the people listed in the Bible.

Through reading, we can learn the fascinating thoughts of people who have lived thousands of years ago. The Psalms of David were his daily journals on his journey with God. He did not know his words would be included in the canon of the Bible. Job cries out to God and yearns that his words be written in a book that would have enduring value. He pictures the latter as an engraving in rock, lasting forever (Job 19:23,24 and in a commentary from: An Exposition of Prayer Old Testament, Volume 2, page 808 by Dr. Jim Rosscup, 2011).

The more I studied, the more I wanted to search. I discovered many Bible scholars called Psalm 139 a great prayer. In praying to understand this great Psalm, I decided to ask God to reveal to me how He had worked with me in the layers of this Psalm. This book is the result.

Did you ever wonder what propelled the early church fathers to write? Did you ever wonder why they chose to go against the current of the general thinking of the day? What caused them to put their lives on the line regardless of the consequences? Local authorities burned them at the stake or fed them to angry wild animals. All this happened while people stood around and laughed. We will never know the inner thoughts of these martyrs. But we do know what happened to them because of their faith.

How were these people able to praise God in the darkness? How? Why? I wanted to find out.

Would you like to find out what I discovered? This book will show you the unexpected discoveries I made by observing others, and the surprising experiences God brought into my life. This book is not a solo but a symphony. A symphony that harmonizes with the Great Providence of God.

I refined my own daily prayer journals and compared them to my prayer journals of years past to see the contrast. By doing this, I was able to see the zigzagging patterns of my past. I could see how to connect the dots. I saw how God had taught me His Will and Way in my life. He created circumstances. He allowed these circumstances to weave a golden thread of His Truth in me. This was done in a way that would change my perception and life forever.

This book is about how God taught me that Jesus Christ is the great bloodline - the great thread between all the chapters, in all the books in the Bible which includes the Old Testament and the New Testament. The entire Bible is a great love story.

This is my unique journey that God chose for me. How did I find this path? I found my path by going to His Word, the Bible, daily with prayer. This was my part. God's part was providing circumstances that would touch my heart in such special ways that I couldn't wait to share my answered prayers with others. Sharing the message of hope to others strengthens the hope in us individually. We are all broken vessels.

God has provided everything we need to overcome. His thread of mercy, grace, kindness, and forgiveness is woven by blood all the way through the Bible. He helps all people who come to Him with a humble spirit and a contrite heart. He always forgives. We are precious to God. This is the great mystery that is difficult to comprehend.

I am a broken vessel just like you. I want to share what God has done in me, to me and through me. We are all sacred vessels created by God in His own image. He has given us talents and abilities, weaknesses and thorns in the flesh, good and difficult circumstances, victories and defeats, friends and enemies, all for His glory and according to His Will. His eternal purposes never change! (Heb. 13:8)

God created us with uniqueness including thinking ability,

consciousness, freedom of choice, and the ability to reflect (Ps. 139). That part of us—this little eternal house—stores all our thoughts, words, and actions and we must live in the little house we have built forever (Prov. 28:7).

Freedom of choice is our own responsibility and each choice is filled with eternal consequences. Choosing to spend time gleaning with humble prayers the principles contained in the ancient Scriptures—the Bible—God's Mind is our way to find the special path that God has chosen for us.

God's covenant to us is His Holy Spirit to help us better understand the Mind of God. His Holy Spirit instructs, comforts and convicts us of sins, and anything else hindering us from being the best possible person we can be.

Prayer is the bridge God provides for us to communicate with Him, and share with Him our failures, wounds, brokenness. When God reassures us how precious we are in His sight, His unfailing love for us, and His faithful promises, our thoughts turn, and we do not continue believing Satan's lies (Ps. 32).

Prayer allows us to make moment by moment choices. When we ask God's light to penetrate the uttermost part of our being, Satan flees. God destroys this deep darkness trying to seep into our hearts. The power of the Holy Spirit in our hearts destroys our enemy and transforms us into a new creation. We are constantly being changed by the light of His Word. The powerful privilege of prayer makes this possible (Heb. 4:16).

Christ's resurrection is God's great gift to us. How is this amazing gift possible? When we accept Jesus Christ as our Savior, His death on the cross and His resurrection, when we choose to be buried in the waters of baptism, we die to our old self. Then, we can rely on God's great promise that His Holy Spirit will lift us up when we face our cross each day.

God the Father lifted Christ into the heavenly realms to reign with him. He has provided the Holy Spirit to lift us up when we face our crosses daily. The Holy Spirit will ultimately lift us up on our last day. His thread of mercy, grace, kindness and forgiveness is woven by blood all the way through the Bible. His promise makes this possible, so we can spend eternity with God worshipping Him, the great I AM.

I hope you decide to go on this journey with me, so you too can experience how—"The Joy of the Lord is Our Strength"—the same as the saints of old.

Introduction
THE BIG PICTURE

We can't see the big picture if we are inside the frame.

When I began this book, I was inside the frame. I opened my Bible, read, meditated and asked God to help me understand what I was reading. What does this all mean? Why was I born? Why am I here?

In this book, I will share what God has done to me, for me and with me. How God transformed my life, provided all the money, friends, circumstances and resources to equip me to be an instrument to reach others with the Good News of our Beautiful Savior, Jesus Christ.

I came from very humble roots. One of my first vivid childhood memories was when I was five years of age. I had a best friend, Billy, who I spent a lot of time with. One day I heard his younger brother had wandered away from home, fell into a lake and drowned. I heard about this, but it never registered until I saw Billy's younger brother in the tiny casket in the family's living room. That is how it was done in those days. At eighty-six, I can still remember that little casket and the deep questions I asked God: Why do people die?

My mother was a very strong believer in God and the Holy Bible. My Daddy was not a believer. Mother quietly lived out her conviction that the Bible is alive, God's promises are true, and that He will show us the best way to live. Her favorite scripture was, "Every word of God proves true. He is a shield to all who come to him for protection. Do not add to his words, or he may rebuke you and expose you as a liar" (Prov. 30:5-6) (NLT).

Daddy finally accepted Jesus Christ as his Savior when I was fourteen. When Mother died at seventy-one, her last words were "And we know that

God causes all things to work together to those who love God, to those who are called according to His purpose. " (Rom. 8:28) (NAS).

Daddy was devastated when Mother passed away, but God did work together in Daddy's life and sent him a wonderful wife who loved him dearly. They lived together another seventeen years before Daddy passed away at eighty-six years of age. So, it was no surprise that I grew up believing the Word of God—the Holy Bible is alive and powerful today.

When my husband died, I was completely devastated. In my quiet times, as I walked through this deep grief, as I opened my Bible, a certain passage always grabbed my attention. "The time is surely coming, says the Sovereign Lord, when I will send a famine on the land—not a famine of bread or water but of hearing the words of the Lord" (Amos 8:11) (NLT).

I read it and thought about it in wonder. Now twelve years have rolled by and as I reflect on the turmoil surrounding us now in 2019, I am stunned. People get so caught up in the chaos of modern life. Somewhere between the contrast of this fast- paced world and thoughts of purpose, meaning and wisdom can fill the mind and we are puzzled. However, the answers are in the Bible.

If the description above reflects you, my hope is what I am about to share will guide you closer to God—seeking all answers prayerfully from the Bible. I will show how God has guided me and I have faith He will do the same for you. The journey begins with a decision to open the front cover of your Bible. There is a reason why the Bible is still the number one best seller after thousands of years.

Psalm 139 Amplified Bible AMP

O Lord, you have searched me [thoroughly] and have known me.
You know when I sit down and when I rise up
[my entire life, everything I do];
You understand my thought from afar.
You scrutinize my path and my lying down,
And You are intimately acquainted with all my ways.
Even before there is a word on my tongue [still unspoken],
Behold, O Lord, You know it all.
You have enclosed me behind and before,
And [You have] placed Your hand upon me.
Such [infinite] knowledge is too wonderful for me;
It is too high [above me], I cannot reach it.
Where can I go from Your Spirit?
Or where can I flee from Your presence?
If I ascend to heaven, You are there;
If I make my bed in Sheol (the nether world, the
place of the dead), behold, You are there.
If I take the wings of the dawn,
If I dwell in the remotest part of the sea,
Even there Your hand will lead me,
And Your right hand will take hold of me.
If I say, "Surely the darkness will cover me,
And the night will be the only light around me,"
Even the darkness is not dark to You and conceals nothing from You,

But the night shines as bright as the day;
Darkness and light are alike to You.
For You formed my innermost parts;
You knit me [together] in my mother's womb.
I will give thanks and praise to You, for I am
fearfully and wonderfully made;
Wonderful are Your works,
And my soul knows it very well.
My frame was not hidden from You,
When I was being formed in secret,
And intricately and skillfully formed [as if embroidered
with many colors] in the depths of the earth.
Your eyes have seen my unformed substance;
And in Your book were all written
The days that were appointed for me,
When as yet there was not one of them [even taking shape].
How precious also are Your thoughts to me, O God!
How vast is the sum of them!
If I could count them, they would outnumber the sand.
When I awake, I am still with You.
O that You would kill the wicked, O God;
Go away from me, therefore, men of bloodshed.
For they speak against You wickedly,
Your enemies take Your name in vain.
Do I not hate those who hate You, O Lord?
And do I not loathe those who rise up against You?
I hate them with perfect and utmost hatred;
They have become my enemies.
Search me [thoroughly], O God, and know my heart;
Test me and know my anxious thoughts;
And see if there is any wicked or hurtful way in me,
And lead me in the everlasting way.

PART ONE
God's Omniscience

Omniscience is defined as knowing everything. God is self-existent and no other is. God is the Supreme Being of the Universe. As the Highest King, God has absolute will over everything and does whatever He pleases. God is all knowing. For God to be sovereign over His creation and all things whether visible or invisible He must be all knowing. His omniscience is not restricted to any one person in the Godhead—Father, Son, and Holy Spirit are all by nature omniscient.

1 Kings 8:39; Ps.139:1-4; 15-16; Isa. 46:9-10; Matt. 9:4; 10:29-30; 12:25; Mark 2:6-8; John 1:47-48; Acts 1:24; 1 John 3:20

CHAPTER 1
From Chaos to Calm

O Lord, you have examined my heart and know everything about me.

—Psalm 139:1 NLT

MY CHALLENGING RELATIONSHIP WITH MY FATHER

I didn't really know who my father was until God started revealing this to me little bit by little bit after my mother died in March 30, 1977.

At that time, we lived in Winston-Salem, North Carolina. Harold was co-pastoring a church and I had recently secured an accounting job. Mother and I were very close. Throughout all the years, she had written, or we talked on the phone nearly every day. Her painful bone-cancer illness devastated me. Daddy called saying we needed to come to San Diego, California very soon to tell mother good-bye. We immediately made the long drive from North Carolina to California.

After my painful visit of telling Mother goodbye, with her last words still reverberating in my soul: *Jane Ann, remember to read Romans 8:28. God will make all things work together for good for all those who love God and are called for his purpose.*

The next thing I remember, Harold was already in the car. I lingered to tell Daddy good-bye. I reached over to give him a hug. He turned his back to me. He walked away. Now forty years later as I write this, I can still feel that sting of rejection. As the following months rolled by, as I attempted to call him and talk like I was accustomed to talking to my mother, Daddy told me, *Do not call me. I will call you when I am ready to talk.* I wondered if there would ever be healing and understanding of my earthly father.

REFLECTING ON MY RELATIONSHIP WITH MY FATHER IN 1959

My memory again returned to a scene eighteen years earlier.

On a hot, dry, day in Santa Ana, California in October 1959, as I rolled over in bed, I could feel the damp pillow soaked with my tears. The room was dark. I was alone. The darkness, the confusion and the chaos that was hovering over us seemed to be lasting forever. This contrast was jarring after our months of excitement as we had planned the great adventure of taking our five small children on a missionary journey to New Zealand.

While I was deeply thinking about this, suddenly without warning, I heard loud, angry voices coming from somewhere in the house. I listened intently.

Harold, what have you done to my daughter? Your selfish, adventurous dreaming has pushed her over the edge! Now, what are you going to do? Jane Ann and these five little children are so confused!

I recognized my father's voice. After a long pause to catch his breath, my daddy continued his raging accusations at Harold ending with, "*We are going to take the children with us until you can get your act together!*"

The door slammed. I strained to listen, but silence continued, and I rolled back on my pillow and cried. Did I know this would reoccur eighteen years later, making my feelings appear as brittle *again?*

God never gave up loving my father and working with me to desire to understand this complex man. God was at work. In the following months after mother's death, my daddy required hospitalization and doctor visits. He could not drive. A gracious widow at church faithfully took care of him. In a short time, they were married.

When I met Faye for the first time, I was stunned. She looked like my mother. She was extremely affectionate, kind and gracious just like my mother. Then, I remembered mother's last words. I cried and thanked God. Daddy caused me much pain and suffering, but God gave me this daddy for a special purpose and God wanted me to love him.

Our Relationship in 1980 to 1993

As the years unfolded, Daddy's raging anger persisted. Although he had served mightily in many church capacities over a long period of time and had a gracious second wife who loved him dearly, his raging anger continued to control him.

Years later I discovered he had continued the raging against the church that had loved him over many years. He was also not content with his marriage partner Faye. He continued to write contentious letters to members of the church.

When I discovered this, I was angry, embarrassed, hurt and puzzled. I felt a deep responsibility to try to help in any way possible. This church had faithfully supported our family in many mission endeavors. They were good through and through people.

I called one of the elders to express my sadness. His answer left me speechless! He'd said, *we love your father. He served this church in many capacities. He was a soul winner and personally baptized over one hundred people. He was the church treasurer. He was the custodian after he retired. We respect him. We deal with many elderly people here. Many times, physical conditions cause them to be caught up in anger. We just tell the congregation to love him and to remember all the good things that he has done and to ignore the letters he sends.*

After the call, I sat down and sobbed. I had never known anyone with that kind of love. This was especially powerful to me because of his position of being an elder in the church. We had suffered many times because of elders. This was such a contrast. This was so refreshing. I cried tears of joy!

After this phone call, I decided to try to change his thought processes. I convinced him that he needed to share his life story with his grandchildren. Daddy was delighted to do this. So now after fifty-eight years, I can share with you his life story.

The Life Story of Loran Richard Critchlow

The name Critchlow is Anglo-Saxon, from Chuchis (cross) and Hiawe (hill) and means dwellers on the hill by the cross.

3

The background of the Critchlow heraldry shield is divided into four quarters—two red and two silver.

The red stands for boldness, daring, blood and fire—a burning desire to spill one's blood for God and country.

Silver denotes purity, justice and peace.

The martlet is always painted without feet as a symbol to the younger sons that they must trust their wings of virtue and merit to rise in the world and not to their legs, as they have little or no land to put their feet on. In ancient times, the lands of the fathers were given to the oldest son, and the lands of mother to the next son. By the time the younger sons were reached, there was little land left for them.

The harp symbolizes purity, depth of character, and exaltation. By its own soft, impressive sounds, it appeases many a storm of the human soul.

The mantle is red and silver. It is an ornamental design by the artist to represent a textile covering on the helmet worn for protection. A sword would become tangled in it.

BIRTH AND EARLY YEARS

Daddy was born February 1906, in Terre Haute, Indiana near the banks of the Wabash River in the southwestern part of Indiana. He was the oldest child of a family of eight. His father was a factory worker. They all lived in a four-room house. They had an outhouse and got water from a well. He was born at home.

Daddy had a strong sense of family responsibility. At an early age, he had a paper route. As he got older, he continually increased his ability to help support the family. When he was a young adult, he delayed marriage until he was twenty-four because he felt responsibility to help his parents. He was very fond of his mother. She was a great positive influence in his life. She was a hard worker and had much responsibility taking care of the needs of the children. However, she was not physically strong and suffered depression. She carried with her the weight of losing both of her parents very early in life. She missed her mother who had died when she was a child. There were five children. After her death, the father had adopted out all five children in five different families scattered around. He chose to never see any of them again. He followed that choice until he died. This really bothered my Daddy.

MY REFLECTION ON MEMORIES OF MY GREAT-GRANDFATHER WILLIAM RAY

I remember as a small child, getting in the family car and traveling a great distance to see my daddy's grandfather. When we arrived at great-grandfather's house and daddy knocked on the door, his second wife answered the door. Daddy told her who we were, and we wanted to see our great-grandfather. She went away and came back. She firmly replied that he did not want to see us. We drove home in silence. Afterwards, Daddy never did talk about this again. So, I am sure he felt extreme *rejection*.

EARLY MARRIED LIFE

My parents were married June 1930. They eloped in Paris, Illinois. Daddy worked for a bakery delivering bread. Mother worked as a clerk in a department store. In January 1931, his dad died. His mother was left with three children: a teenage boy, Rex; a girl ten, Ella Mae; and a girl eight, Ruby.

In July 1931, my daddy's mother died and left my parents to raise the three children. My parents found suitable housing and furniture to meet their needs. Afterwards, Daddy increased the intensity of his ability to support his newly acquired family.

I was born into the family on January 1933 on a cold, snowy, icy day. Daddy's first mention of me in his family history said I cried every time he held me. He said one night as a newly born baby, I cried and could not sleep. He tried to comfort me. He could not get me to stop crying. Then he frantically turned on the radio to music. I stopped crying and fell asleep. Daddy mentioned how much Ella Mae and Ruby enjoyed taking care of me.

In January 1935, my brother Jack was born. He was a sickly child and needed much care. Mother took a long time to recover from Jack's birth. So much of my early care came from Ella Mae and Ruby. Not too long after Jack was born, Ella Mae got sick. Her cold, sore throat and pneumonia turned into severe heart issues. Soon after she died. We were all in a state of shock!

I was told Ella Mae took care of me much of the time. Her death traumatized me. Ruby was seriously depressed for a long time. Once we could not find her. After hours of hunting, we finally found her in the back of a dark closet crying. We were all living on the edge of chaos and turmoil.

Daddy's teenage brother Rex was very confused. He quit school in his senior year. Daddy then purchased a small grocery store with a house next door in a nearby community to provide a job for Rex. He then trained Rex to manage the store.

One day as a toddler, I got out of the house and fell down the front porch steps. Although I had hit my head, I decided to get up and go see my new playmate. As I ran across the railroad tracks to her house, I did not stop to look for a train. When I crossed the railroad tracks, a train was coming. My playmate's mother was in her yard pushing her daughter in a swing. When she looked up, she heard the blast of the train's eerie horn. She saw me. She dashed to the railroad track, grabbed and rescued me. The scar I now carry on my forehead reminds me of that day.

We lived in that house for several years. Rex met the love of his life. We always called her Tot. They got married. They moved away. Daddy invited Mother's dad Robert Lee Collins, who was of Native American ancestry, to manage the store.

In a short time, we learned my grandfather was an irresponsible alcoholic. Daddy sold the grocery store and the house. We moved to 811 South Third Street in Terre Haute, Indiana where we lived all my elementary school days.

One of my vivid memories of those years around 1940, was waking up in the middle of the night and hearing my mother screaming, "No! No!"

Daddy had come home drunk and had ripped Mother's new red long-sleeved blouse with gold buttons into shreds. I never did understand why. However, not long after that incident, Mother started wearing a beautiful new fur coat. This coat was in mother's closet in 1977 after she died.

THE GREAT DEPRESSION YEARS

Daddy continued to focus his energy trying to support his family. However, this was during the Great Depression. Many people were without jobs. Daddy's cousin, Vern was manager of a large grocery store in Terre Haute. He told Daddy when he had arrived to work that day, two hundred people came into the store with burlap bags, filled them with groceries, and walked out. His cousin called the sheriff. The sheriff did not come. He was afraid to do anything.

People had to stand in lines a mile or so long just to get a loaf of bread and a pail of milk. Banks closed. People lost all their money. Factories closed. Some men committed suicide.

I remember as a little girl going to answer the screen door. A tramp was there asking for food. I unlocked the door and invited him in. He told me to go tell my mother he was here. He said she would not want him to come in. Our house was near the railroad tracks.

Men would hitch a ride in a boxcar, then stop along the way to get their meal of the day. Mother always made them an egg sandwich. Daddy continued his work at the bakery. Even with his limited education, Daddy's determination allowed him to become the manager of Bell Bakeries with seventy-five employees during the World War Two Era.

Although Daddy smoked two or three packs of Camel cigarettes every day and continued drinking, mother focused on her little family at home: Ruby, Jack and me.

Mother took us to church every Sunday. We rode the bus transferring several times along the way. At the final stop, we walked to the small white frame church building in the northern part of town and entered via a little front porch.

Mother never complained. She instead turned her concerns over to God. Many times, I had seen her in the porch swing reading her Bible with the tattered front cover and underlining her favorite passages. One passage she always quoted to me was, *I have hidden your Word in my heart that I might not sin against You* (Ps. 119:11). Mother's greatest joy was teaching her second grade Bible class.

Often at night I hid a flashlight under my pillow, so I could read my Bible before going to sleep. My dream was to marry a preacher, and while

I was the least likely candidate, I prayed earnestly that God would send a preacher my way.

When I was ten years old, I decided I wanted to be baptized. For some reason, all baptisms were at night. I think it was because it took a long time to prepare the baptistry. Buses didn't run at night. So, Daddy agreed to drive us to church. He refused to go inside the church. Instead, he waited outside in the cold grey Plymouth for us to return.

One of the elderly women at church told us that Daddy had been in Bible school in her class when he was eight years old. She said at that time the church was small and met in a widow's home. She said that she was praying for Daddy. She thought he was angry with God because he had lost so many people in his life that he loved dearly. She thought if we prayed and waited quietly, he would come back to God. She gave us a hug. We left.

Much later when I was fourteen, Daddy accepted Jesus Christ as his personal Savior, and was baptized. Afterward, he quickly turned his thought patterns to the beautiful awareness that Jesus Christ, who created everything, accepted him just as he was. This thankful power allowed God to give him the necessary abilities and energy to quit smoking, quit drinking alcohol and start down a new path of allowing God to use his abilities and efforts to serve others. This attitude continued in this season of his life until the love of his life was struck with painful cancer and died.

Afterward, despite my daddy's deep feelings of sadness, grief, depression and anger rushing in trying to overwhelm and destroy him, the gracious, loving leaders of the church, his devoted second wife, family and friends did not abandon him. They stood by him and surrounded him with loving support. They covered his severe wounds of sadness, grief and rejection with bandages of gentle small acts of respect, kindness, effective listening, acknowledging his pain and suffering until the very end of his life.

God is a Merciful God. He also experienced deep grief when He turned his back and could not watch His Only Son die on the cruel cross! God knows our hearts! Won't it be a great surprise to all of us to have the capacity in Heaven to see the true loving, gracious, merciful character of God? I think we will be stunned to learn how many times God had saved us from ourselves on our journey on earth!

The foundations of law and order have collapsed. What can the righteous do? But the Lord is in his holy Temple; the Lord still rules from heaven. He watches everyone closely, examining every person on earth (Ps. 11:3-4) (NLT).

Christ is the visible image of the invisible God. He existed before anything was created and is supreme over all creation, for through him God created everything in the heavenly realms and on earth. He made the things we can see and the things we can't see —such as thrones, kingdoms, rulers, and authorities in the unseen world. Everything was created through him and for him. He existed before anything else, and he holds all creation together (Col. 1:15-17)(NLT.)

When we were utterly helpless, Christ came at just the right time and died for us sinners (Rom. 5:6)(NLT).

So now we can rejoice in our wonderful new relationship with God because our Lord Jesus Christ has made us friends of God (Rom. 5:11) NLT).

REFLECTIONS

———————————————

1. What secret activity are you afraid that God knows and sees?

2. Have you given thought to this in the past?

3. Do you believe that Jesus Christ is God in human flesh?

4. Reflect on Colossians 1:15-20 in three or four different translations. This is easy to do on ww.biblegateway.com. You can look up passages or key word studies.

5. Do you believe that Jesus Christ died for your sins?

6. Do you believe you have no sin? We all sin and need forgiveness.

7. Spend time this week reflecting what God has revealed to you after your private, secret, daily Bible studies.

8. Start a prayer journal and record your thoughts as you reflect on this study.

CHAPTER 2

The Invisible Hand of God

You know when I sit down or stand up.
You know my thoughts even when I am far away.
—Psalm 139:2 NLT

As a child, I was very curious and full of questions. One day while sitting on the floor beside my toy box—an old discarded leather trunk—I pulled out a mirror. As I stared at myself in the mirror, I wondered, where was I before I was born? Is there another world inside? Why is Daddy always angry? Why does Mother go to her room, close the door and cry? What happened to my friend, Ella Mae? Why did she die? I miss playing our little games together. Why?

In my childish way, I was always trying to figure out what life was all about. Reflecting now, I realize even at my young age, God was preparing me for a special purpose. God had kept increasing a curious, questioning spirit in me and I remember wanting to know why!

One day, many years later while cleaning out a file cabinet, I discovered a tiny file stuck in the back of the drawer. Opening the tattered file, I found a little booklet announcing the winner of the First Prize of the Poets Study Group in Terre Haute, Indiana. Inside was a poem I had written at sixteen years old. Here is the poem.

THE DESERTED GRAVEYARD

The stars shone down so clear and bright,
Through the darkness of the eerie night.
The pale moon high up in the sky,
Cast a glance with his wistful eye
On that deserted graveyard where
All was as still as a solemn prayer.
The wind gently blew around vaults of stone
Leaving scents of earth and sweetness to be known.
Far from view and shadowed by a tree,
Quiet, lonely, and peaceful as could be,
Was one neglected slab of stone,
On it was engraved, "Identity Unknown."

After reading this poem, I asked myself the question, who am I? I then turned to my Bible hoping to find out who God thinks I am. I found my answer in the book of Psalms:

> *When I look at the night sky and see the work of your fingers—the moon and the stars you set in place—what are mere mortals that you should think about them, human beings that you should care for them? Yet you made them only a little lower than God and crowned them with glory and honor* (Ps. 8:3-5 NLT).

As I read this poem and my Bible verse, I reflected on the many dark moments of my life and I wondered why.

As a child, I learned to accept my speech impediment. My life had been full of humiliation and embarrassing moments.

One of those experiences happened when I was in the fifth grade. After all these years, I still remember that moment vividly. My mind trailed back to that time. I can still see myself sitting in that crowded classroom. I remember squirming and looking down the aisle at the blur of students. I looked at my watch. I looked at the teacher as she sat at her desk ready to pounce like a big ugly spider. Her glasses were so thick her eyes looked like dirt specks at the end of a telescope. She focused on me, "Jane Ann, it's your turn."

My cheeks were blazing, and when I stood up, my legs felt like jelly but somehow I got to the front of the class. I turned around and looked at the other students, but my mind went blank. How could I talk without stuttering?

"Jane Ann, we're waiting. Speak up!" The teacher had said as she tapped her desk with her pencil. Tiny vibrations irritated my lips. Panic gripped me. Frantic struggling only produced more of the uh—uh sounds.

Most of the kids were snickering. Jerry jabbed Jim. Tom grabbed his throat choking and almost swallowed his bubblegum. Betty Jo and Mary Jane giggled.

The teacher looked sternly at the students, cleared her throat and said, "Jane Ann, if you knew it, you could say it. Go to your seat. You'll have to stay after class today and pick up a progress report for your parents."

As I look back now in 2019 to my childhood, I consider the speech impediment as a great gift from God. It has taught me some very valuable lessons. However, it took many years for me to see this.

As we go to the Bible to see what God thinks, let's read Ex. 4:10-16 (NLT)

> *But Moses pleaded with the Lord, "O Lord, I'm not very good with words. I never have been, and I'm not now even though you have spoken to me. I get tongue-tied, and my words get tangled. Then the Lord asked Moses, "Who makes a person's mouth? Who decides whether people speak or do not speak, hear or do not hear, see or do not see? Is it not, I, the Lord? Now go! I will be with you as you speak, and I will instruct you in what to say." But Moses again pleaded, "Lord please! Send someone else." Then the Lord became angry with Moses. "All right." He said. "What about your brother, Aaron the Levite? I know he speaks well and look! He is on his way to meet with you now. He will be delighted to see you. Talk to him and put the words in his mouth. I will be with both of you as you speak, and I will instruct you both in what to do. Aaron will be your spokesman to the people. He will be*

your mouth-piece, and you will stand in the place of God for him, telling him what to say. And take your shepherd's staff with you and use it to perform the miraculous signs I have shown you."

After studying what God thinks, I learned that all my speaking challenges were created by God. Therefore, if I rebel about this, it is rebellion to God's plans for me. As God told Moses He would teach him how to deal with this issue, I also had to listen to God. I researched how people throughout the ages have dealt with this. I made some very fascinating discoveries. Gerald R. Mc Dermott wrote a book called *Famous Stutterers*. Some of his twelve inspiring stories include Aristotle, Winston Churchill, Annie Glenn and John Updike. In other resources I learned Joe Biden and John Stossel also shared this issue.

The character lessons I have learned through the years are many. I learned to trust in God more. I learned to actively listen more. I have more empathy for people going through painful experiences. It has helped me to not speak angry words. It has caused me to write my thoughts in a daily journal to God. It has caused me to rely more on God's direction in my life.

Looking back, it is understandable why I had such an intense desire as a child to pray, and to beg God to lead me to a strong believer of the Good News. I prayed that God would direct me to a Christian husband and a proclaimer of this Good News. I also prayed that God would control my tongue.

Did God answer my prayer? While I had been praying all those years to marry a strong Christian man, and a proclaimer of the Good News of Jesus Christ, God had been working all along to answer my prayers. God had been working in the heart of a little eight-year-old boy preparing him to be that person I longed to meet someday.

After a challenging incident, when our children were teenagers, this is a story that Harold told some of our children. I included this story in my book, *God's House! Beautiful! Let's Go!*

It was August 1938 in southern Indiana. I was eight years old. About three miles from our home was an old pond. The coal mine took its water from this pond to operate its boilers.

I was taught at a very early age not to go to this pond because it was crawling with snakes. Periodically my dad and the other men would take their guns and dynamite and go down to this old pond to try to get rid of as many snakes as possible. But I also knew that around the banks of this old pond were the most beautiful cattails to be found within miles

One day I decided that I wanted some cattails. I knew that my dad had told me not to go. I had been to the pond with the men when they were killing snakes. But I said to myself, "I'm old enough, and if I take the necessary precautions, nothing is going to happen." So, I went to the bank of that old pond. I got a good-sized club, rolled up my pants legs, and slowly walked in. I thrashed the water with that club. I was doing great. I'd go along and cut cattails, and before long I had a whole armload.

The first thing I noticed, however, was that my club was in the way. I really didn't think now there was any need to exercise any caution. So, I threw my old club away and went ahead cutting cattails. As I continued cutting, suddenly, I felt a great pain in the calf of my left leg. I raised my leg up and there was a big old water moccasin hanging on my leg! I knew enough about snakes not to run home. Even now after all these years, I can still remember vividly an eight-year-old boy struggling not to run home, but to walk very slowly and to remain calm. By the time I reached home, I was quite ill. I was feverish. The snake's venom had already done its work.

I remember the days and nights that followed this incident. I can still recall the room where I rolled and tossed in pain, and I can still see my bed. Many times, I have looked back through the years and remembered that scene. I have asked myself many times the question, "Why?"

After many years I realized that this incident in my life was a blessing—a divine blessing. I have been able to look back and ask why, and then understand, why you and I sometimes do the things we do in life.

Each of us knows sin is a terrible thing. It separates us from our God. It damns our eternal soul. Once we have been bitten by that serpent, it can be fatal.

Why then armed with all this knowledge, do you and I continually, habitually, seek after those things that we should not seek after and do? As I look back to that August day, I thought what I really wanted was cattails.

Now I know what I really wanted was to say to my dad and to all those men who had warned me, "You don't know what you are talking about. I wanted to say to them, I am the exception. I can take my club. I can arm myself with precautions and I can engage in this sin and nothing is going to happen to me."

When Dad saw me coming home, he gave me an affectionate hug and quickly called the doctor. He did not punish me. Later he said he knew that I had learned my lesson, and I would now respect snakes.

Why did you tell us that story, Dad?

I just wanted you to know that I still love you. You are all unique snowflakes. You are all very special in your own way.

That's how God feels about us. He loves us just as we are. He knows that we are weak and need help. He is always ready to forgive if we ask him. God knows that if we reject him, and go ahead and sin, we will suffer painful consequences.

However, if we decide to change directions and ask for God's help, he will always give us the direction and strength to walk through our struggles to overcome our unwise choices.

So, just like my painful snake bite, sin has painful consequences. As God heals us when we come to him, we learn to respect the goodness of God and the wisdom in his word, the Bible.

One by one the children got up from the table, gave their Dad a hug and silently walked away.

Reflecting on this story, I see it as a parable—showing how God's plan is always perfect instruction, if only we decide to take it. Straying from

God's guidance always leads to dark places, just like the bite of the snake in the story above. The child rebelled against his father's instruction and then reaped the dire consequences. The child's father didn't scold—he gave his son the gift of loving compassion.

Are we any different than the rebellious child? Sometimes we aren't any different at all, and we too fall flat on our face. Christ redeems us when we ask for forgiveness (Ps 32).

Reading the Bible—the Living Word of God—is powerful. As I reflect on "Word" in the Gospel of John, I must go to the Greek word which is "Logos." Let's read.

"In the beginning was the Word, and the Word was with God. He was in the beginning with God. All things were made through him, and without him was not anything made that was made. In him was life, and the life was the light of men. The light shines in the darkness and the darkness has not overcome it" John 1:1-5 ESV.

"And the Word became flesh and dwelt among us, and we have seen his glory, glory as of the only Son from the Father, full of grace and truth" John 1:14 ESV.

The English expression for *Word* was translated from the original Greek word called *Logos*. Word Studies in the New Testament by Marvin R. Vincent says:

"The Real Meaning of Logos in John

"As Logos has the double meaning of thought and speech, so Christ is related to God as the word is to the idea, the word being not merely a name for the idea, but the idea itself expressed. The thought is the inward word."

Yes, God's Word is alive and transforms our lives. As we blindly stumble along, God gently tries to open our eyes. When we stumble and fall, and painfully take the time to ask for guidance, God shows us how he gently saved us from ourselves. Then, we drop to our knees in prayer, thanking him for his unfailing love, mercy and grace.

When I reflect now on this, my thoughts go to this Psalm.

Let all that I am praise the Lord; with my whole heart, I will praise his holy name. Let all that I am praise the Lord; may I never forget the good things he does for me. For his unfailing love toward those who fear him is as great as the height of the

17

heavens above the earth. He has removed our sins as far from us as the east is from the west. The Lord is like a father to his children, tender and compassionate to those who fear him. For he knows how weak we are; he remembers we are only dust. Our days on earth are like grass; like wildflowers, we bloom and die. The wind blows and we are gone—as though we had never been here. But the love of the Lord remains forever with those who fear him. His salvation extends to the children's children of those who obey his commandments!

The Lord has made the heavens his throne; from there he rules over everything (Ps. 103:1-2, 11-19 NLT).

REFLECTIONS

_____

1. How do you feel when you think that God knows your thoughts?

2. Do you wonder why the God who created everything would take the time and effort to know your thoughts?

3. Read Psalm 8:3-5 in several translations. Pray that God will give you understanding as you read.

4. Spend time this week reading and reflecting on this Psalm

5. Record your thoughts about this in your journal.

6. Do you have a painful story to record? Has Satan lured you into a snake-filled pond to get cattails?

7. Read Luke 15:11-24 and 11-19.

8. Record your thoughts in your prayer journal.

9. Read John 1:18. Pray, meditate and write in your prayer journal.

CHAPTER 3
Surprised by a Sudden Storm

"You see me when I travel and when I rest at home. You know everything I do."

—Psalm 139:3 NLT

My husband and I were teenage sweethearts. We were married young. He was nineteen and I was seventeen. This was during the Korean War. Harold joined the Air Force. He was stationed in Biloxi, Mississippi. Both of our families were well rooted in Indiana, so this was a big adventure for us. We had no idea where this journey would lead. We just sang, "Trust and Obey," packed our Bibles, and then moved on to Mississippi, next Texas, and then on to Ohio and then California.

June 1957—When our fourth daughter, Catherine was born, we lived in a ranch house in California, not far from Death Valley. The nearest town was eight miles away and was called Four Corners.

This little town consisted of four businesses including a gas station and a small grocery store. The settlement where we lived was an abandoned ranch where farmers raised alfalfa. During a period of draught, the two little houses were rented to tenants.

Harold was working in research and development at Edwards Air Force Base. We had recently been transferred from Dayton, Ohio. This was the only housing available at the time. During Harold's off duty times, he filled the pulpit of a little church in Boron several miles away. We had only one car.

The hospital was in Mojave about sixty miles away. We had no telephone service. The man who rented the other ranch house had no car, only an old motorcycle. My mother always came to help during the birth of our children.

Harold and I had both prayed much about what would happen when I went into labor. We just lived and prayed. When my time came, God performed a miracle!

On a bright, busy Sunday morning, we all climbed into the 1956 Ford station wagon and headed for church in Boron. It was a great service. A young man answered the call of Jesus at the end of the service. He made his confession of believing that Jesus Christ is the Son of God—God clothed in human flesh.

The little church in Boron met in a store front and we had no baptistery. The church in Barstow forty miles away had a baptistery. Barstow church leaders were kind and gave us permission to use their baptistery. We immediately drove to Barstow.

This was a long but beautiful day. We came home to a wonderful meal I had prepared on Saturday—a large pot of beef roast with potatoes, carrots and onions. When dessert time came, I gobbled down a luscious plate of strawberry shortcake with yummy whipped cream. Then it happened! The labor pains started hard!

Harold began to panic! He remembered he had forgotten to fill up the gas tank after our long trip to Barstow. We both got into the station wagon. Mother stayed behind to care for Deborah, Diana and Janice.

Harold tried to hurry, but I told him to go slower and watch the bumps in the road, because each bump brought on another labor pain. We stopped to get the gas.

I waited in the car. I prayed! Oh, how I prayed!

Did God answer my prayer? Yes!

We arrived at the hospital. The nurse took me directly to the labor room. Before I could comprehend what was happening, and before Harold had completed signing my admission papers, little Catherine was born!

After all our concerns, God allowed Catherine to be born on the only day of the week Harold was home with the car—and it was Sunday, the Lord's Day!

> *But may all who search for you be filled with joy and gladness*
> *in you. May those who love your salvation repeatedly shout,*
> *"The Lord is great!"* (Ps. 40:16) (NLT).

Our Desert Lake House
1958 - 1959

After waiting so long to find a suitable home for our growing family, we finally found a newly built house in a small community near Boron, called Desert Lake. I especially enjoyed my beautiful kitchen. The walls were cocoa brown. The cabinets were a soft yellow. I made yellow ruffled curtains for the windows.

My heart sang whenever I walked into the living room to the bench in front of the organ that Harold had purchased for me. I loved to play the organ in the afternoon when the children were playing outside. Music always soothed my restless soul.

One day, Harold insisted on packing up the family and driving to the desert in search of white quartz stones. We made several trips until we had collected a huge pile. Harold then laid all the gold-flecked stones in stone masonry fashion. Harold created a full wall on our garage front. It was striking when the desert sun lit the lines of gold flecks in the stones.

After we were settled in our new home, I discovered I was pregnant again. This pregnancy turned out to be quite different from the others. From the beginning, I had morning sickness, fainting and then bleeding. The doctor gave me strict instructions to get bed rest, so I would not have a miscarriage.

It was very difficult to get bed rest and care for the needs of our two-year-old and three other children. A neighbor lady, the wife of Harold's co-worker, brought her two little children to our house daily to help. Harold had been studying the Bible with her entire family for several months. She had been baptized and was eager to talk to me about her new Bible studies.

Soon my parents decided to move from Farmersburg, Indiana to California. After several weeks, they moved in with us until the birth of our son, John. With their help, I received the needed rest and I carried our little son to full-term. The labor was extremely long and painful. At one point, the pain was so intense and unending that I wondered if I was going to die.

However, when the healthy, amazing little boy was placed in my arms, I praised God for this great gift and his unending love, mercy and patience with me during my ordeal. I remember seeing the doctor frustrated. I think he expected this experience to be quick like Catherine's birth. He tried talking to me to get me to relax. He told me that he was the youngest child in his family, the only boy, and had four sisters. I saw his facial expression change to a little smile. He delivered both of my babies on a Sunday— Catherine in June and John in December.

My parents moved from our home to San Diego when John was three weeks old. After we were comfortable with our new schedule and re- organizing our home, Harold and I finally had quality time to spend with each other. Hours of conversation in the evenings with coffee and dessert, we connected. It was wonderful!

One Monday evening in March 1959 while all the children were asleep, Harold and I sat on the couch, held hands while Harold prayed. Afterwards, Harold looked deeply into my eyes and said that he had something very important to discuss with me. He said "First, I want to tell you a story about my childhood.

When I was a little boy, my grandmother had a picture hanging in her living room of two little children walking across a hanging bridge. The wind was blowing, the lightning was flashing and directly behind them a beautiful angel stood with outstretched arms ready to catch them in case of danger.

I have been thinking about that picture a lot recently. Last week I read Hebrews 1:14 again. It tells us that God sends angels to help and care for those of us who are to receive his salvation. Also, in Hebrews 13:2 I read, 'Do not forget to entertain strangers, for by so doing, some people have entertained angels without knowing it.'

I have been thinking a lot about what happened this past Sunday evening at church. There was a crippled man who came late for church and sat on the very back row. He listened so intently. When my sermon was over, after I had greeted a few people, I made my way over to where he was standing. He seemed to be waiting to talk to me. I asked him if he had just moved to Boron. He told me he had been to a clinic in Los Angeles. The doctors had told him he had a terminal condition. He said he was on his way home to Alaska to die.

I can still see his face as his eyes deeply pierced mine. Mr. Derr, 'You must continue preaching. You must keep on. You really need to reach out to people. God needs you and wants you to stay in the pulpit.'

He then asked me to take him to the truck stop at Four Corners so he could catch an eighteen-wheeler and then work his way to Alaska. We talked in the car on our way to Four Corners. He did not want to speak of his illness. He kept the conversation going by continually encouraging me to keep preaching the Good News of Jesus Christ. His last words keep echoing in my head. "You must keep on preaching. God Bless. It was good talking to you."

He got out of the car and walked toward an eighteen-wheeler parked in the parking lot. I saw him talking to the driver. When he came back to the car, he told me the driver was taking him to Portland, Oregon."

After Harold finished telling this story, he paused, and looked at me. I could see his painful expression. He then continued.

"How could this stranger have known the tremendous struggle I have been experiencing about whether to resign from my present job and then begin preaching full-time? Do you think I have entertained an angel from God to help with my decision? Here was a stranger who appeared for a moment and now he vanished from my sight. I wonder?"

I thought for a moment. I hesitated. I gazed into his troubled, serious eyes and then replied, "Yes, Harold I believe the crippled man was an angel. Now what shall we do?"

At this time, Harold worked at NASA Space Flight Facilities at Edwards Air Force Base. He was in the Research Laboratory working on the engines for the Atlas ICBM and Thor IRBM Ballistic Missiles. It was a very challenging job that required many hours. He enjoyed the challenges and excitement of preparing the initial work that eventually led to sending a man to the moon. However, he worked mostly nights and it was very difficult to sleep during the day with five active children in the house. His real passion was studying the Bible and preaching at the friendly little church in Boron.

Boron was in the Antelope Valley region of the Mojave Desert. Most of the people who lived there came from Oklahoma during the Great Depression. Borax deposits were discovered in and around the area of Boron. Soon, the large borax mining industry was established. This mine provides nearly half of the world's supply of refined borates. It was a great contrast to the other employer--the aerospace industry. This mine provided jobs for most of the people in this little church.

One of the main leaders worked at this mine. He was married and had a teen-age son. They lived in a beautiful concrete block house. This family started out living in a tent. As they collected money and supplies, they built a room, then they lived in that room. When we met them, their house had been completed. It had three bedrooms, a kitchen, dining room, living room and a bathroom. They were debt-free. We learned much from these good, simple, friendly, humble people.

The song leader was the son of a single mom who was in the Air Force. She had been stationed in Korea. Her son, Malcolm Parsley, later went to Korea as a missionary. Sixty years later, Malcolm still serves in Korea as a great servant of the Lord with his wife and family.

When our son John was four months old, we attended a missionary revival near Pepperdine University. The missionary from New Zealand, who addressed the audience that night spoke about the great opportunity for the message of the Good News to be preached in that country.

Harold's heart was stirred and he felt that God wanted him to make a change. When he learned two other families our age plan to go as a team, we started praying together about this challenge.

Harold resigned his position with the space program. He quickly received his financial support for the mission work. We sold our house and our household effects. We packed our essentials in steel drums to go with us on a ship to Dunedin, New Zealand on September 7, 1959. Everything was moving along smoothly.

Pepperdine University had scheduled their annual Missionary Lectureship about this time. We looked forward to attending and connecting with many of our missionary friends stationed in foreign countries.

My parents had agreed to take care of all the children, so we could go. Just a few days before this lectureship and our scheduled departure, the elders of our sponsoring church announced to Harold that we could not go. Why? We were not told why!

We were emphatically told no. You cannot go! Since our financial support came entirely from a foundation that supported only missionaries and the funds had to be distributed through a sponsoring church, the decision of the elders was final.

Afterward they recommended that Harold enroll in Pepperdine until we could decide on our future. Yes, indeed, our future had been shattered in ten thousand different pieces in a matter of minutes.

After this news, Harold and I tearfully prayed and then decided to attend this lectureship as we had originally planned.

At the lectureship, I had just left the large auditorium after Harold and I had listened to a missionary tell about his exciting experiences in France. He was no stranger of France. As a soldier in World War Two he had learned to love the people.

When he returned as a missionary, his wife was in a wheel chair. The people were very compassionate. As the family walked in the marketplace, many people came to help her. This handicap gave them the opportunity to tell the people about Jesus Christ. Bible classes in their home, led to many students accepting Christ and were baptized. I was jolted to learn about their many hardships and wondered why they were so full of joy. It was difficult for me to reconcile pain with joy.

After this lecture was over, I walked alone in the foyer toward the next class taught by a missionary wife from Nigeria. As I was trying to process our circumstances, make sense of all the pieces in the light of what I had just heard from the last lecture. An old acquaintance stopped me. She immediately asked me when we were leaving for our New Zealand missionary trip.

My lips quivered as I tried to speak. I could feel my cheeks becoming hot. My legs started shaking. My body tingled. I felt myself fall to the cold marble floor. I looked up. Faces with puzzled expressions looked down at me. The room went black. Everything else was a blur until I woke up at home in bed.

"Why did you let this happen, God? Why?" The bed shook as I sobbed.

My eyes appraised the room, but I was confused. I became focused on the fact we were living in a condemned house. The owner of the house had received an order from the local authorities they were going to tear the house down soon. Since this rental house was empty and we desperately needed housing, she agreed to let us live in this house until the final order came to destroy it.

My next thought was, *"Why am I alone? Where are my children? I miss my children so much. It feels so strange to be alone. Where is Harold? The house is too quiet."*

The bedroom door slowly opened, and four-year-old Janice peeked inside. I could see into the open hallway. It was light. I know it must be daylight.

"Come in Sweetheart," I said as I propped my pillow so I could see.

"Mommy, Mommy! See my picture! I drew this picture in Bible class just for you!" she said as she proudly held up the picture so I could see.

"Is that your handprint?" I asked.

"Yes, Mommy, we all drew a picture of the nails in Jesus' hands when he was on the cross," she said slowly as she looked down at her picture with the hand colored red. "Our Bible class story today was about Jesus on the cross."

"I am so glad that you went to Bible class. This is so precious," I said as tears formed in my eyes, and I motioned for her to come closer, and then gave her a tight hug. Janice's eyes beamed as she said, "I like Vacation Bible School!"

"Who took you?"

"A lady from church. Bye, I'm going outside to play with my new friend from VBS," she replied as she ran out closing my bedroom door.

About this time Harold came into the room and gently touched me. "How's my sweetheart doing today?" He wore a broad smile. "We had a prayer for you today in the Chapel at Pepperdine. I know you will be better soon."

He knelt by my bedside. He began "Let me sing to you one of the songs we sang this morning. 'I know the Lord will find a way for us. I know the Lord will find a way for us. If we walk in heaven's light, shun the wrong and do the right. I know the Lord will find a way for us.'" He stood up, bent down and kissed my forehead.

After he stood up, he quietly put a new book on the bed beside me. After he left, I looked at the book. It was a copy of *The New Testament in Modern English by J. B. Phillips.*

The next morning, as I started my daily Bible study and casually opened the New Testament Harold gave me, this Scripture stared me in the face:

Forgiveness of fellow man is essential

> *For if you forgive other people their failures, your Heavenly*
> *Father will also forgive you. But if you will not forgive other*

people, neither will your Heavenly Father forgive you your failures (Matt. 6:14-15).

Put your trust in God alone.

Don't pile up treasures on earth, where moth and rust can spoil them and thieves can break in and steal. But keep your treasure in Heaven where there is neither moth nor rust to spoil it and nobody can break in and steal. For wherever your treasure is, you may be certain that your heart will be there too! The lamp of the body is the eye. If your eye is sound, your whole body will be full of light. But if your eye is evil, your whole body will be full of darkness. If all the light you have is darkness, it is dark indeed!

So, don't worry and don't keep saying, 'What shall we eat, what shall we drink or what shall we wear?' That is what pagans are always looking for; your Heavenly Father knows that you need them all. Set your heart on his kingdom and his goodness, and all these things will come to you as a matter of course (Matt. 6:19-34).

Several days passed. Nothing changed. The darkness still hovered over me. I missed being with my children so much. I was especially concerned about my nine-month-old baby boy.

My thoughts returned to that dark bedroom. I was so alone. Harold and the children were outside. The phone rang. I answered the phone. The lead pastor of a neighboring church said that he had been praying for me. He had been to the Pepperdine Lectureship and heard that I was sick. Some had called it a nervous breakdown. He told me that the Word is our anchor, our hope and then he said, "Cast all your care upon him, for he cares for you."

There was a moment of silence. Then he continued, "Repeat this after me. It is from 1 Peter 5:7. "Cast all your care upon him for he cares for you." He then insisted that I repeat this for a couple more times. He told me that I could also find this in Psalm 55:22. He then had a short prayer before saying goodbye.

After our conversation, something happened to me. Those words rolled over and over in my mind chasing out everything else. It was a new joyful song that invaded my mind. Soon it changed my entire perspective.

A few days later in my time alone with God, I prayed for wisdom to move forward. As I was turning the pages of my New Testament, the page opened to 1 Peter 3 and these phrases of certain verses boldly pierced my soul. *Learn to be humble and to trust.*

In the next line I read,

> *You younger members must also submit to the Elders. Indeed, all of you should defer to one another and wear the "overall" of humility in serving each other. God is always against the proud, but he is always ready to give grace to the humble. So, humble yourselves under God's strong hand, and in his own good time he will lift you up. You can throw the whole weight of your anxieties upon him, for you are his personal concern (I Peter 5:5-7).*

When I recalled my father's words of rebuke, I realized his thinking was flawed by his perception of my security. However, I had agreed in the beginning to support Harold in his decision to do mission work. That was a commitment we had made together as a team. So, now with God's help, together, we will overcome these present challenges!

For the next couple of weeks during my private time with God, I read many Scriptures about baptism. It was so much easier to understand in The New Testament in Modern English.

Thinking back to my baptism at ten years of age, I became increasingly doubtful I had really understood what the baptism really meant. I wanted to be sure of my relationship with God and Jesus Christ. I decided to be baptized again. In the Spring of 1960, the lead pastor of the church in Santa Ana, California baptized me.

Every day I got a little better. It wasn't long until my mother-in-law, Susie Derr, whom I called Mom, arrived in May. She packed all our clothes in suitcases. She also arranged for our other meager possessions we had packed in steel drums be shipped to Terre Haute, Indiana. She covered up the New Zealand shipping labels with fresh Indiana tags. Indiana was our birth state. She and Pops still lived in the same neighborhood where Harold and I first met.

While packing, I discovered a letter. When I recognized it was on the official church stationery, I was curious. It was dated April 2, 1960. I opened the envelope. It was addressed to Harold from the lead pastor of the church in Santa Ana.

> *I am putting on paper the recommendations the elders asked me to convey to you. I put them in writing because memories sometimes fade—mine as well as other people—and in your present critical crisis all of us want to have the same memories and a perfect understanding.*

The elders recommend and urge the following:

1. *That you place Jane under a doctor immediately. This may include both medical and psychiatric.*
2. *They recommend that you immediately give up your school work and seek employment in industry. This recommendation is no reflection on you; it is simply out of a recognition that Jane's condition will make mission work and local church work practically impossible for you for some years.*

I remember how distraught the pastor was when he came to our house. He and Harold spoke quietly. I had not read this letter before.

Our lives were never the same after that moment.

REFLECTIONS

---

1.   Reflect on the thought that God knows everything that you do.

2.   Do you think God really cares when you experience a very painful tragedy?

3.   Do you have difficulty forgiving someone who has hurt you?

4.   Read Psalm 55:22 and 1 Peter 5:5-7 and pray for God to give you understanding.

5.   Now read 1 Peter 5:7 in context or read 1 Peter 5:5-7. The new thought here is focused on humility and forgiving others.

6.   Now read Luke 11:1-4. Then re-read verse 4 *forgive us our sins as we forgive those who sin again against us.*

7.   Reflect now on someone who you have not forgiven. Pray that God will help you to forgive that person.

8.   Read Acts 2:32-41.

CHAPTER 4
The Dawn of a New Day

"You know what I am going to say even before I say it Lord.
You go before me and follow me. You place your hand of
blessing on my head. Such knowledge is too wonderful for
me, too great for me to understand."

—Psalm 139:4-6 NLT

SUMMER 1960

After we arrived in Indiana, a series of amazing events took place. A perfect house for our family became available right across the street from Harold's parents. God provided the funds so we could purchase the house. Harold immediately started working with his dad in the family business—the blacksmith shop making ornamental iron and fencing. After we moved into our new home, I could look out my kitchen window and see the home I had lived in with my parents before Harold and I had met. When I scanned the neighborhood, I began to remember these precious moments Harold and I shared during our courtship days.

While it was a balmy spring morning, and my new environment felt peaceful and secure, I could not stop thinking about California. It was a difficult effort to control my thoughts. I vividly remembered the days I was in the depths of depression. However, one memory kept peeking through--the phone call from the pastor telling me to repeat over and over a Bible verse. Then afterwards, he kept telling me that God cares about me.

"I hate to do dishes!" I grumbled out loud while submerging my hands into the hot sudsy water. I fished out a fork and surveyed the piles of dirty dishes yet to be done. The song "My God and I" could be heard in the background playing from the stereo. I felt my face flush with anger listening to those words—they contradicted how I felt at that moment. The beds were unmade, the laundry room had dirty clothes piled high. The living room was cluttered with toys and newspapers and our sick baby was in the nursery. I felt tears fill my eyes and run down my cheeks. I need you God! Where are you?

Loud screams coming from the front of the house caught my attention. I ran to the front door, opened it, looked down at the screened-in front porch floor, and saw six-year-old Janice lying face-down on the floor. She had fallen headfirst over the spring action riding horse she and four-year-old Cathy were riding. As they rode the range together, the spring broke loose and threw them both off. Upon inspection, I could see both were okay—just minor scrapes. A hug chased their frightened feelings away and they returned to playing with something else.

I returned to the dirty dishes in the kitchen. The music from the stereo had changed. 'There is a Balm in Gilead that Heals the Sin Sick Soul' filled the air. This song is one of my favorites, but I couldn't hear it. My mind was deep into the thoughts of California.

My hand slipped on a wet plate— it crashed to the tile floor and shattered into tiny pieces around my feet. It seemed a metaphor for my life—shattered to pieces. My sobbing returned as the painful memories flooded my brain. Suddenly my mind went blank. I could no longer bear the pain of those memories.

The front door opened and then slammed shut. It was my mother-in-law.

"Janie, I had a few extra minutes this morning. I decided to bake you a couple of pies for lunch." Mom could see my tears.

"What's the matter?" Mom placed the pies on the table. "Is John getting worse? Did his temperature go up again?"

"Oh, he's better. I just broke a dish."

"That's silly to cry over a broken dish, honey. It can always be replaced." Her eyes surveyed the kitchen with dishes piled. "By the way, Janie, I'm not busy at all today. It would be a very good time for me to do some of your laundry and ironing." Mom proceeded to the laundry room and filled a

33

huge basket with dirty clothes. "Better have sandwiches today for lunch. It's almost time for Harold to be home." She then slipped out the back door with a huge basket of laundry in tow.

I stopped to pray, "Thank you God for reminding me You are still here. It is so comforting to know that Harold's Mom and Pops are just across the street. They treat me like their own daughter. What would our life be now if she had not come to Santa Ana, California, packed our belongings and brought us home with her? Mom and Pops even arranged for a loan for us to buy the house just across the street from them. They were certainly an answer to our prayers."

A Tribute To Susie Derr

There shall never be another
Like my second mother.
She's always there
To share my every care
And lend a helping hand
Whatever the demand
Her love and devotion
Is deep as the ocean
Yes, I've been twice blessed
With a mother that's best;
And then another
Like my second mother
Though miles and years may part
She'll always be dear to my heart.

Jane Ann Derr

That night I rolled and tossed in bed. Sleep eluded me. I listened. The house was silent except for the clock striking eleven. Everyone was asleep. I crawled out of bed and walked into the living room. I grabbed my Bible from the nearby bookcase and sat on the couch. As I opened my Bible, I remembered the joy that I received as a child when I secretly read my Bible at night when everything was quiet. I remembered my unquenchable thirst to study the Bible all by myself.

I decided that this would be a great time for me to continue my studies when my family was asleep. I then wrote the following poem and returned to my bed.

THE ANCHOR OF THE SOUL

Loved ones come and loved ones go;
The Word of God abides forever.
Friends come, and friends go;
The Word of God lives forever.
Happiness comes, and happiness goes;
The Word of God delights forever.
Success comes, and success goes;
The Word of God challenges forever.
Fortunes come, and fortunes go;
The Word of God provides forever.
Houses come, and houses go;
The Word of God stands forever.
Good health comes, and good health goes;
The Words of God endures forever.
Memories come and memories fade;
The Word of God lasts forever.
The seasons come, and the seasons go;
The Word of God is forever.
Earth and heaven shall vanish away;
The Word of God shall remain forever.

While the children were in school, Mom kept John and Cathy at her home, so I could rest. I used this alone time to study God's Word and pray. Mother was pleased with my interest in studying the Bible. She sent me a copy of The New Chain Reference Bible containing Thompson's original and complete System and Bible Study. This Bible contained a wealth of information to quench my never- ending questions. I eagerly waited for each time to be alone to study my Bible.

Early on I learned the value of keeping daily journals, which I later turned into prayer journals. Journaling helped me to stay focused. My many interruptions and pressing household duties caused many distractions and kept my thoughts from being laser focused on God's Word.

Soon we learned a nearby church needed a pastor. We prayed about exploring this opportunity, and then wrote to someone we knew was wise. We sought his counsel about wise choices. We continued our daily Bible study together with many agonizing prayers linked together with lengthy discussions. Harold and I both trusted that God would lead us. The person we had sought counsel never responded. Harold moved forward in faith and accepted this position. We both felt peace after our decision.

Months later a letter arrived. It was from the man we'd written to for advice. The letter is below:

> *I am inclined to suggest that you run the business and preach when the opportunity presents. Your own peace of mind will be maintained much from how well your family is getting along. It rejoices me that Jane Ann is doing so well now, and likely one main reason is her feeling of security and well-being. She will live on a narrow margin the rest of her life probably; therefore, most of your own happiness is wrapped up in what is necessary to provide her security.*
>
> *God be with you in your decision.*
>
> *Most affectionately,*

Did God listen to our prayers? Did the providential Hand of God delay this letter? I believe God was answering our prayers for His Will in our life!

After a few days, Harold was appointed the pastor in this friendly, active congregation near our home. In a matter of a few weeks, we adjusted to our new schedule. It was such a joy to be able to be with a loving group of people. They enjoyed singing! We would go to one of the member's homes every Sunday evening after church service and sing. Then we would laugh, eat, and share stories. We praised God for our new life!

This is a poem I wrote for the church bulletin in 1961:

GOD'S WAY

My Lord tells me in pages old,
The only treasures I may hold
Are those laid up in Heaven?
Those I've laid up in Heaven?

Tell me, My Savior, in that city so fair,
How can I know my mansion waits there?"
I love you so dearly and want you to know
That where you are, I want to go.
In simple terms that I might see
My Lord spoke gently unto me,

"I was hungry, and you gave me meat,
I was a stranger and you washed my feet;
Sick and in prison and you came to me,
Naked and you clothed me free."

When did I a stranger see?
And came and ministered unto Thee?"
My Lord just smiled and softly said,
"The least of these my brethren you have fed.
Your love for them I did perceive
And you did it unto Me, as you did it unto these."

So always deal kindly with your struggling brother;
Smile and remember that God gave you each other.
So, handle each precious one with loving care,
When God gives you days that are fair.

For who knows your tomorrow
May bring loneliness and sorrow.
The billows may rage, and the waves may roar,
And your safety to the Eternal Shore

> *May very well depend on that brother,*
> *And how you dealt with one another.*
> *(Matt. 20:26-28; 22:36-39; 25:31-40)*

ONE OF MY JOURNAL ENTRIES FOR 1961

We participated as a church and read through the entire Bible—the Old Testament and the New Testament in a year and Harold preached the Sunday evening sermon about our weekly Bible studies. At the end of the year we were able to have sixty-five people on the honor roll that completed the readings. We were all blessed by the reading of the Scriptures and amazing things happened.

HOW GOD TAUGHT ME TO MEDITATE

> *Sustain me, and I will be rescued;*
> *then I will meditate continually on your decrees.*
> *—Psalm 119:117 NLT*

God taught me the beauty and power of meditation while I was recovering from the most depressing time in my life. While on this journey, I wrote an article that was published in Christian Woman, May 1962 Volume 30 Number 5. Here is the article:

> *I don't like to do dishes! I suppose it's because doing dishes for a family of seven sometimes seems like a never-ending task. But one day I realized what a wonderful opportunity I had been missing to glorify God. It dawned on me that in these depressing moments the devil was better able to pry his way into my heart and cause me to dwell on unrighteous thoughts.*
>
> *"You are tomorrow what you think today" is a very true statement, and the scriptures bear this out. "And now dear brothers and sisters, one final thing. Fix your thoughts on what is true and honorable and right and pure and lovely and admirable. Think about things that are excellent and worthy of praise." (Phil. 4:8) (NLT).*

Pondering these things in my heart, I remembered a statement that Martin Luther made, "The devil flees before the sound of music almost as much as before the Word of God."

"And whenever the tormenting spirit from God troubled Saul, David would play the harp. Then Saul would feel better, and the tormenting spirit would go away." (I Sam. 16:23 NLT)

Good thinking is a matter of conditioning. What better way could be found than rooting out of the mind evil thoughts with hymns of praise and devotion to God as David did for Saul.

My decision was made. I moved our portable record player into the kitchen and collected an abundant supply of inspirational Christian hymn recordings. Every time I started the dishes, I also started the record player. Soon I found myself singing "My God and I" as I stacked the plates in the dish rack. Within a few short weeks I found myself looking forward to "singing the dishes away." As I sang and meditated on the beautiful thoughts expressed in each song, the time just seemed to fly. My dishes were done, and I was on my way rejoicing. Gradually my changed attitude reflected in my other daily activities, and soon my husband and children noticed the change and were quite pleased.

Within a short time, when I knew the words by memory, I could better dwell on the beautiful sermons in song ringing daily in my ears. I could better understand why Paul said, "I will sing with the spirit, and I will sing with the understanding also" (1 Cor. 14:15). I realized how in the quiet and familiar surroundings of our home I could truly glean the lessons portrayed in each song. Now when my three-year-old son and my four-year-old daughter wiggle my song book during worship services, I am better able to capture a portion of the spirit and understanding of the songs being sung, and, in turn, I am better able to keep my spirit in tune for the rest of the worship service.

> *Since we know not what good or ill tomorrow may bring
> let us redeem the time and store up all the Bible truths that
> we have capacity for that we may be able to withstand in the
> evil day when trials and temptations come our way. Let us
> learn to completely put our trust in God who will fight for
> us when we are unable to fight. "Casting all your care upon
> him; for he cares for you" (1 Peter 5:7).*

Although we were not permitted to go to New Zealand as missionaries on September 7, 1959, God allowed us to arrive in Ghana, West Africa, on September 7, 1963. How precious is the mighty Providence of God? To God be the glory!!

Recently, I read an article in Christianity Today saying the first time in over a century, less than half of New Zealanders call themselves Christians. (www.christiantiday.com 10/29/15).

However, today in Ghana West Africa Christianity has spread abundantly with churches, Bible Seminaries and hospitals. Additionally, many Ghanaian missionaries are being sent out to over twenty other countries including America.

When we pray and start out, God determines our steps pointing us in the direction that will be most beneficial to the Glory of God. So, don't be downhearted when things do not go your way, because God in His timing, will prevail. He alone knows the best pathway for our life. We only find this out by going to His Word daily, with a humble heart, expecting change and embracing it.

> *"I knew you before I formed you in your mother's womb.
> Before you were born, I set you apart and appointed you as
> my prophet to the nations." (*Jer. 1:5 NLT)

MY PRAYER ADAPTED FROM Psalm 56:1-13

Heavenly Father have mercy on me.
When I am afraid, I will put my confidence in You.
You have seen me tossing and turning through the night.
You have collected my tears and preserved them in Your bottle!
You have recorded everyone in Your book.
The very day I call for help, the tide of battle turns.
My enemies flee!
This one thing I know: God is for me!
I am trusting God—oh, praise His promises!
I am not afraid of anything mere man can do to me!
Yes, praise His promises.
He will surely do what He has promised.
Heavenly Father, thank You for Your help.
For You have saved me from death, and my feet from slipping,
So that I can walk before You Lord, to the land of the living.

In Jesus Name
Through His Precious Blood
Amen

REFLECTIONS

---

1. Think about God's omniscience. Omniscience is defined as knowing everything. God is self-existent and no other is. He is the Supreme Being. He has life within himself.

2. Read these Scriptures and reflect on them.

3. Record your discoveries in your journal.

4. Read Jeremiah 1:4; Psalm 56:1-13.

5. Write your own prayer from these Scriptures.

PART TWO
GOD'S OMNIPRESENCE

The term Omnipresence means all-present. This term means that God is capable of being everywhere at the same time. It means His Divine presence encompasses the whole of the universe. There is no location where He does not inhabit. God is present everywhere at once. Yes, He is everywhere at the same time as though all-enveloping and His Divine law is omnipresent. God is simultaneously present with all His attributes or essence at once everywhere.

CHAPTER 5
The Mercy of God

I can never escape from your Spirit! I can never get away
from your presence! If I go up to heaven, you are there; if I
go down to the grave, you are there. If I ride the wings of the
morning, if I dwell by the farthest oceans, even there your
hand will guide me, and your strength will support me. I
could ask the darkness to hide me and the light around me
to become night—but even in darkness I cannot hide from
you. To you the night shines as bright as day. Darkness and
light are the same to you.

—Psalm 139:7-12 NLT

For God has imprisoned everyone in disobedience so he could
have mercy on everyone.

—Romans 11:32 NLT

Yes, this mercy is for the Jewish people, the Israelites. Yes, this mercy is for the Gentiles. Yes, this mercy is for me! Yes, even me! It is so difficult for me to comprehend this. Can you comprehend this? I cannot. So, I asked God to help me to understand and believe this:

"Christ is the visible image of the invisible God. He existed
before anything was created and is supreme over all creation,
for through him God created everything in the heavenly

realms and on earth. He made the things we can see and the things we can't see—such as thrones, kingdoms, rulers, and authorities in the unseen world. Everything was created through him and for him. He existed before anything else, and he holds all creation together. Christ is also the head of the church, which is his body. He is the beginning, supreme over all who rise from the dead. So, he is first in everything. For God in all his fullness was pleased to live in Christ, and through him God reconciled everything to himself. He made peace with everything in heaven and on earth by means of Christ's blood on the cross. This includes you who were once far away from God. You were his enemies, separated from him by your evil thoughts and actions. Yet now he has reconciled you to himself through the death of Christ in his physical body. As a result, he has brought you into his own presence, and you are holy and blameless as you stand before him without a single fault. But you must continue to believe this truth and stand firmly in it. Don't drift away from the assurance you received when you heard the Good News. The Good News has been preached all over the world, and I, Paul, have been appointed as God's servant to proclaim it. —Col. 1:15-23 NLT.

I think that King David also had a difficult time comprehending this great truth about God's mercy, everlasting love, compassion and grace. He expressed his thought about this in the following Psalm:

O Lord, our Lord, your majestic name fills the earth! Your glory is higher than the heavens. You have taught children and infants to tell of your strength, silencing your enemies and all who oppose you When I look at the night sky and see the work of your fingers—the moon and the stars you set in place—what are mere mortals that you should think about them, human beings that you should care for them? Yet you made them only a little lower than God and crowned them with glory and honor. "You gave them charge of everything you made, putting all things under their authority—the flocks and the herds and all the wild animals, the birds in the sky, the fish in the sea, and everything that swims the ocean current. O Lord, our Lord, your majestic name fills the earth. —Ps. 8:1-9 NLT

My hand slipped causing my prayer journal to fall on the floor. I bent down to pick it up. I burst out laughing when I noticed what was written on the opened pages—details of an incident in the Fall of 2013. At that time, I'd considered myself to be a confident and self-reliant woman. Why, I'd just published two books and was still living alone in the house my late husband had remodeled and expanded. My confidence had been soaring.

I'd gone to the Public Library in Cumming, Georgia for a special book sale. Once you entered the designated area, a librarian handed you a large bag with the instruction to fill the bag as full as you wanted and then only pay five dollars for all those books. I'd purchased four of these fully loaded bags.

Thoroughly delighted in my treasures and having unpacked and organized into subject, grabbed one and sat down in my favorite reading chair positioned in the exact spot in the sunroom where my late husband had passed away.

A cup of tea sounded perfect to have while perusing this book in hand. I went to the kitchen and made a cup. I'd only just returned to my chair when a loud boom suddenly got my attention. Then, the sound of rushing water coming from the kitchen caused me to dash into that direction. Water was gushing out from the cabinet under the sink. I stooped down, opened the cabinet door and searched for the cut-off valve, but to no avail. The water continued rushing out. My ankle-length cotton muumuu was drenched. It badly weighed me down. Standing back up was difficult.

I managed to make my way to the phone. Certainly, one of my friends will come to my rescue. Unfortunately, after attempting to reach six different people, no one answered. Suddenly, I realized this was the week of our annual Fall Fair. I inhaled and exhaled deeply.

Afterwards, I dialed my son's number who did answer. I told him my predicament. He replied, "Mom, what are you thinking? I live in New York City! You have ADT Security. Just push the button and the fire department will come."

John stayed on the phone until the firemen arrived, who easily cut off the water.

These firemen were gracious and kind—quieting my fearful words and reassuring against my embarrassment. When I realized my reaction to the burst pipe was irrational—emotionally fueled chaos—all previous beliefs in my confident independence were dashed.

A disaster recovery company came at the insistence of the firemen and promptly set up their equipment to dry up all the water. The noisy forty machines ran even after the men left. They insisted the machines must stay on for about two weeks to dry up all the water. I was told this was important to prevent mold spores. My heart sank when I watched them drive away.

The next morning my son phoned. "Mom, what were you thinking last night? What is going on with you? This incident seemed to paralyze you. To change your thinking remember this: Keep Calm and Carry On. This message was told to the British People during World War II by Winston Churchill. I'm going to get you a bookmark to remember this."

After reading this 2013 journal entry, I spent much time thinking, reflecting, praying and reading. I reflected on my son's three-hour conversation that day. I was stunned about my reaction to this incident. After again reflecting all these events, I got a fresh thought.

I had prayed many times that God would direct my thoughts in writing this book. God was teaching me now that He wants me to rely on Him and Him alone and not on second-hand knowledge of other people.

As my husband Harold would always teach: God has no grand-children. You are either a child of God or you are not. This is a journey that everyone must take alone. You cannot rely on the second-hand knowledge and experience of others and expect to receive God's first-hand power. God works with and in each of us individually. He uses our unique God-given talents to hopefully work together harmoniously to be a great symphony—His Church.

It was hilarious God taught me that lesson while I was loading up on huge bags of books written by Bible scholars and servants of His instead of going directly to His Word. So, I opened my dusty Bible and wrote this poem:

IN THE VALLEY OF DECISION

When confusion and chaos rattle your brain,
What do you do to remain sane?
Do you make that choice another day?
And just get up and walk away?

Do you blame and complain and cause a commotion?
to your Facebook friends across the ocean?
Or, do you stop and look for another way?
Yes, what does the Bible say?

So, pull your dusty Bible off the shelf,
Putting God's thoughts into your inner self.

Look up to God and pray,
Trusting He will show the way.

God sees the great enemy called sin
is powerfully battling to come within
So always remember the old rugged cross
And God's incomprehensible loss.

So, this is the secret for you and me
The only way to be set free.
Now my eyes were opened, and I could see
God's beautiful love for you and me.

When I look at that blood-stained cross
I see the peace and not the loss.
Christ chose the pain
So, I could forever gain.

Now death is no longer dark
and a gloomy question mark.
It's a secret place with God alone
As I travel to our Heavenly Home

the threat of death is overthrown.

Jesus Christ has set us free
Shout for joy the victory!

Jane Ann Derr
Joel 3:44; Zech. 14:1-9; Hosea 4:1; Col. 3:14; Rev. 22:3

Yes, what was I thinking? I am sure God laughed out loud when he watched me. God has a real sense of humor. He put me in that situation to teach me a great lesson on pride; the importance of humility, and moment by moment relying on Him directly for my thinking. I will then act differently.

God wanted me to delight in the power of the process as the vibrations and energy of the transforming force of the Holy Spirit was working in my life. However, at the time, all of God's silent workings in my life were truly hidden from my sight. I really got the message after I read this journal several years later.

Much later, I realized that God was showing me the process that powerfully rests in fragile vessels of human flesh. God performed miraculous changes in me just as He performed miracles in Moses, Elijah, and Christ and this same power can be in me if I allow it to happen. Humility, surrender and trust are the great secrets. Our free choice and our valley of decision.

A dear friend who has passed on, Ed Taylor, said many times, man is a forgetful creature. This thought has stuck with me over many years. The Bible reports that Moses, Job and the Apostle John wrote down messages from God. (Ex. 17:14; Job 19:23-27; Rev. 1:1-2)

If I had not kept journals along the way, I would not have remembered all the ways that God has led me over the course of eighty-six years of experiencing life. Choose to take the time to record journals. You do not know the trials you will be experiencing in the future. You will need the power of your journals to allow you to remember good thoughts of God's blessings for you as Satan continually shouts accusations (Phil. 2:4-8; 3:13-14; 4:13).

This same power will rest in you if you stop and take the time to read your Bible and pray for guidance. Keep a journal. Record God's answer.

"With your very own hands you formed me; now breathe your wisdom over me so I can understand you. When they see me waiting, expecting your Word, those who fear you will take heart and be glad. I can see now, God, that your decisions are right; your testing has taught me what's true and right. Oh, love me—and right now!—hold me tight! just the way you promised. Now comfort me so I can live, really live; your revelation is the tune I dance to. Let the fast-talking tricksters be exposed as frauds; they tried to sell me a bill of goods, but I kept my mind fixed on your counsel. Let those who fear you turn to me for evidence of your wise guidance. And let me live whole and holy, soul and body, so I can always walk with my head held high." (Ps. 119:73-80 MSG)

REFLECTIONS

---

1. Read Psalm 139:7-12 and Romans 11:32

2. Ask God to help you understand.

3. Focus on the mercy of God; then reflect on a time in your life that God rescued you from yourself.

4. Write your thoughts in your prayer journal.

5. Write a poem about how you make choices and contrast that with how God wants you to make a choice.

6. God wants us to record our thoughts in a journal. Read: Ex. 17:14; Job 19:23-27; Revelation 1:1-2

PART THREE
God's Omnipotence

The term omnipotence is the quality of having unlimited power. This expression is generally held and only be attributed to the Trinitarian Godhead—Father, Son, and Holy Spirit. This Great I AM can do anything He pleases and corresponds with His omniscience and world's plan.

God's omnipotence and perfect power is free from all actions that do not agree with His essence or attributes. The activity of God is simple and eternal without evolution or change. The range of His power is limited only by His Sovereign Will. God's perfect power uses His perfect knowledge, and wisdom in using His all-sufficient power.

CHAPTER 6
The Eternal God Formed Me

You made all the delicate, inner parts of my body and knit me together in my mother's womb. Thank you for making me so wonderfully complex. Your workmanship is marvelous— how well I know it. You watched me as I was being formed in utter seclusion, as I was woven together in the dark of the womb. You saw me before I was born. Every day of my life was recorded in your book. Every moment was laid out before a single day had passed.

—Psalm 139:13-16 NLT

Every life is woven together by many layers of intricate patterns of circumstances, experiences, doors of opportunity, roadblocks, focus, distraction, habitual thoughts, consistent actions, and continual streams of conflicts, stops and starts, and never-ending failures to meet our intended objectives.

God is always looking for ways to turn our missteps, failures, disappointments and self-made disasters into blessings only He could perform. This reminds me of an experience in my own life that I will never forget. God knew me but showed me that I did not know myself.

THE EVENTS LEADING UP TO MY STORY

When Harold was alive, I felt my one hundred percent focus should be on helping him, being a good wife, a good pastor's wife, supporting him in all his challenges, successes, disappointments and achievements. Then, when he passed away, I had the satisfaction that I did the best I could at every fork in the road. However, with all the busyness, as pastor's wife, church secretary, preparing meals for guests in our home, counseling, home Bible studies, maintaining a second life as an accountant for forty years with forty-mile commutes to and from work left little time and energy for really getting acquainted with my five children, fifteen grandchildren and numerous great-grandchildren.

At the time, I did not realize this great loss, however, God did and pointed me in that direction. Just before Harold passed away, some of the children gathered around his bed to tell him goodbye. At that time, I promised I would complete the book about our missionary journey to Ghana, West Africa.

Afterward, I wrestled with the conflict of dark days of deep grief and contemplating how I would fulfill the promise I had made to Harold. I had promised him I would complete a book about our missionary journey. God rewarded me by allowing all five of our children to share their own personal feelings about those special times for our family in 1963 -1965 in Ghana, West Africa.

This turned into a very exciting project for all of us. It was very healing as we shared our joys and heartbreaks, gains and losses, fears and faith, exciting adventures and loss of familiar pleasures.

Looking back now to that time, I know this was God's great gift to me. Through the years, I had not been able to spend as much quality time with all my children because of the necessity to work in my accounting positions. When I started processing my grief, I realized that loss also.

However, God in His everlasting love, grace and compassion created circumstances, so our children could build a great bond with their dad. I am so thankful for that, because a good father is so important to children. It helped them to see the goodness of their Heavenly Father. Now God was giving me this time. It was so special to work with all the children to put the book together.

On September 2012, exactly six years after Harold passed away and after successfully publishing my second book, *God's House! Beautiful! Let's Go!* sharing how our family coped with Harold's cancer and death, my second daughter Diana, and I sat down to eat lunch at Golden Corral in Cumming, Georgia for one of our special times together to sit, reflect and talk.

At that time, for some unknown reason, I was feeling anxious wondering if something dramatic was about to happen. Diana had just lost her job. Three of her four children lived in other states. Her married daughter, Amanda, with her husband Joseph and two young sons lived in Georgia. Soon they would be moving to Texas.

The day was sunny and warm. The food was especially delicious. As we started our dessert, we were laughing about our crazy adventures in the past. We shared how God had always looked over our foolish choices in His great mercy and rescued us, gently pointing us in the right direction.

This conversation led to the idea that maybe God was providing this time now for us to experience another new adventurous trip. In our excitement, we decided this was the perfect time—a do it now or never time. Immediately, our conversation turned to planning our next adventure. We decided Fall was the best time to see the Northeast. We could also see family and friends along the way. We would leave October 4 and return home about October 18.

God loves to make us laugh—at ourselves! How does He do it? By exposing us to the great contrasts in our lives.

Did I ever think in my wildest dreams, at this late time in my life, I would choose to take a 2,600-mile-two-week trip with my daughter in her new 2011 Ford Fusion Sports car? She was a great driver that could compete with any race car driver. I had completely forgot that obvious fact. My comfort zone was being a very conservative driver. What was I thinking?

Harold was quick to speak words of wisdom in simple to understand sayings. Two of his favorite sayings were:

> *Be careful what you pray; then fasten your seatbelt!*
> *You cannot teach what you do not know.*
> *You cannot lead where you do not go.*

This trip taught me lessons from these two sayings. When I was terrified, I heard voices inside of me quoting God's precious promises from

His Word. When I cried out to God, we were protected by God's army of angels surrounding us.

When my thoughts of concern for Diana (who had only a few days before been diagnosed with severe heart problems) I started to panic and played the what if game. To my surprise, the voice inside of me, started singing this song, *it is well with my soul…. When peace like a river attendeth my way, when sorrows like sea billow roll, whatever my lot, thou hast taught me to say, it is well with my soul.* (Words: Horatio G. Spafford 1873) (Music: Phillip P. Bliss 1876)

If I had not taken the time years before in my life to prayerfully tuck all those Bible verses and hymns in my heart, they could not have come back to me in my time of need and given me peace. These tiny seeds through the years slowly marinated in my mind as they interacted with the Holy Spirit in me. Like yeast in bread. That is what prayerful study of God's Word did to me.

This only happens when we choose to take the time and effort and allow God to do His work in our life. Our times are in God's hand. God gives the breath of life moment by moment. Time is like a river. You can't touch the same water twice because the flow that has passed will never pass again. God gives us the precious gift of freedom of choice. So, it is up to us to believe, trust and act on the promises of God. We must stop, think, and act before the moments slip away and are gone forever.

A few days after our trip of perfect Fall weather, great timing, and exciting events, I was stunned to see on the news, the effects of one of the greatest storms in the history of our nation. Hurricane Sandy struck widespread devastation on the exact places where we had visited just days before. How stunning!

> *Teach us to realize the brevity of life, so that we may grow in wisdom (Ps. 90:12) (NLT.)*

> *I wait quietly before God, for my victory comes from him. He alone is my rock and my salvation, my fortress where I will never be shaken (Ps. 62:1-2) (NLT).*

THE BEAUTY OF UGLINESS

At the age of five, my little friend died. I was terrified. As I matured into adulthood, I read that death is like being in a room with no exits or on a one-way street with a dead-end. We all must die. It doesn't matter who we are, our ancestry, nationality, education, sex, physical appearance, a super-star, unknown person, our wealth or poverty, our good or bad deeds, we all have this one fact to face: *we all will die.* Wisdom teaches us that the earlier we accept this fact, the better our life will be.

My inward trauma at this early age caused me to think about death often. When my mother took me to a little church that proclaimed baptism is the answer, I was baptized when I was ten. This helped me for a while, however I still had this restless spirit wondering if there is more.

Now, I can see God placed these thoughts of death in my mind for His great purpose. As I sit here remembering my past, I am amazed at the many times, God had rescued me from danger and completely changed my pattern of thoughts. This change only happened because of my restless spirit and choice to stop, go to God in prayer, pick up my Bible and beg God to direct me. It was not easy because I came onboard with a stubborn heart, many flaws and a very humble background and with a determination I could make changes by my own effort. Very quickly I discovered I could not!

GOD MADE ME WONDERFULLY COMPLEX

In time, bit by bit, moment by moment God changed my heart through many circumstances, people in my life, and some of my experiences. I have lived in thirty-some different homes in many different states as well as Ghana, West Africa. As a mother of five children, my dream was to stay home and care for each of my children. However, a financial conflict arose: my husband was preaching the Word of God, the needs of the family increased and our income from the church did not cover these financial expenses. Harold and I prayed earnestly how to solve this problem. The little church was composed of beautiful, caring, loving, poor people. They simply could not give more. So, Harold and I chose to resolve this conflict.

I would get a secular job, and he could adjust his schedule to help with the children and household daily chores. In this way, he could continue the work he so dearly loved.

GOD HELPED ME FACE MY ONGOING CHALLENGES

I had stuttering problems, a high school diploma with a major in art and a few months training in a Business College, but no advanced degree. My first real business challenge was in Ghana, West Africa. For us to survive in Ghana, I needed to do all the secretarial work which included extensive reports of our work to all our contributors. The contributors would send funds to our sponsoring church and this church would then send funds on to us. My job was to send timely financial reports to all our contributors and sponsoring church monthly.

One of my challenges was to understand the currency exchange concept. We were required to account for every penny of the working fund and to send financial reports monthly to our sponsoring church. I had no calculator or adding machine, no fax machine, no computer with applications, to do any of the work.

Time was of the essence. Communication was difficult . Mail was transported by ship. We had no telephone service. I depended solely on God to help me to figure it all out.

Did God help me? Absolutely! He helped me every step of the way. He also helped me to homeschool my oldest daughter Deborah in the sixth grade. Yes, she survived and has done quite well. (Incidentally, she has edited this book). This was the beginning of my business career. God is good!

Despite my feeble effort and humble background, in my great need, God gave me on the job training. As the years rolled by, we moved to the Los Angeles area, and I was accepted for a job in bookkeeping. The controller was from my home state of Indiana. He liked me and assumed I could handle the job because of my age.

My first job assignment was to close the books for the year. I had no idea how to complete that task. I did not have any schooling in bookkeeping or accounting. So, I went to the bookstore and purchased a book called, *Bookkeeping Made Simple.* I read part of the book each evening after work.

I took the book to work and hid it in my desk drawer. I worked through each step one at a time until I completed each task. To my surprise, my work was accepted.

My next challenge was to figure out how to balance accounts receivable, payables, bank reconciliations and other reports. I developed a mistake log. Every time I could not balance a report, I would review my mistake log. Next, I would question myself. I would study the situation and question why I made this mistake. In time, I learned I would always make the same type of mistake. So, I effectively used this method to simplify my challenge. This method helped me immensely to not panic under pressure.

My employment journey led to twenty-one different types of jobs. I would not have been able to survive without my daily time of going to God's Word. At that time, my go to Scriptures were always in the book of Proverbs. I would ask God to help me with every task. I enjoyed making daily journals to see how God would respond to my prayers.

The Power of Reflections

At the time of my experiences, my feelings were raw, and I could not see how any outcome would be positive. However, going through my journal years later, I could see the powerful hand of God working. True peace comes with reflective thinking. It takes time to process information. This is the key to the right path. One dose of reflective thinking of a previous journal entry could completely change the path of your life in a positive way! This is what happened to me.

The experiences I faced on the jobs and the forty-mile commutes to work and home in old vehicles with many trials along the way, all strengthened my faith in a very amazing, compassionate, gracious, merciful, magnificent, all-knowing, sovereign God, the Great I AM.

Some of my jobs were: driving forty miles at night in the Mojave Desert to work in a Post Office Distribution Center. My job was to drive a mail truck to the railroad station and load the truck full of one hundred twenty-five-pound mail sacks by myself. Sometimes a crippled man helped me.

I've worked in a blue jean factory, training girls to sew the jeans. I've worked in a company entering data for accounts receivable. I've worked as a full charge bookkeeper for a clothing distributor and a certified public accounting office completing work for clients in Hollywood, Beverly Hills, Long Beach and other areas in Southern California.

In New Jersey, I worked with two companies at the same time—a medical equipment distributor in Cherry Hill, and a retail furniture company in the Moorestown Mall.

In Kentucky, I worked for a civil engineering firm, and then to another certified public accounting firm. In North Carolina, I attended Guilford College for accounting classes, and then worked as comptroller for Winston-Salem Arts Counsel for eight years. Next, I sat for the Financial Principles Exam, and worked for two stockbrokerage firms in North Carolina and in Georgia. In Atlanta, I worked for an electronics/computer distributor for nearly twenty years. I retired at eighty-two after working for a certified public accounting firm for eleven years.

Yes, all these experiences I've faced have strengthened my faith in an amazing, compassionate, gracious, merciful, magnificent, all-knowing, sovereign, eternal, and unfailing, loving God—the Great I AM.

TREES

In Ps. 139:13-16 we learned the eternal God formed us. In other Scriptures, we learn that God compared us to many things. Let's stop and investigate some of these concepts.

God has compared people to many things in the Bible such as a building. (1 Cor. 3:9); Sheep (Isa. 53:6; I Pet. 2:25); Salt and light (Matt. 5:13-14).

In I Pet. 1:24-25 (NLT), we read: "As the Scriptures say, People are like grass; their beauty is like a flower in the field. The grass withers and the flower fades. But the word of the Lord remains forever. And that word is the Good News that was preached to you."

I found twenty-seven verses in the Bible mentioning trees. God taught many lessons using trees as examples. Let's look at some of these verses and focus on the lessons that God used as lessons for us.

GOD COMPARES US TO A TREE

THE WAY OF THE RIGHTEOUS AND THE WICKED

"Blessed is the man who walks not in the counsel of the wicked, nor stands in the way of sinners, nor sits in the seat of scoffers, but his delight is in the law of the Lord, and on his law, he meditates day and night. He is like a tree planted by streams of water that wields its fruit in its season, and its leaf does not wither. In all that he does he prospers. The wicked are not so, but are like chaff that the wind drives away. Therefore, the wicked will not stand in the judgment, nor sinners in the congregation of the righteous; for the Lord knows the way of the righteous, but the way of the wicked will perish." (Ps. 1:1-6 ESV)

In Psalm 1, God compares people to a tree. Let's look at some of the characteristics of trees. First, a tree is a symbol of strength, majesty and beauty. Second, we are planted like a tree. We are planted in Jesus Christ.

(Rom. 6:5) "For as many of you as were baptized into Christ have put on Christ." (Gal. 3:27 ESV)

TREES IN HEAVEN

We learn in Revelation 22 that the River of Life flows from the throne of the Living God and on either side of the river are trees planted. The leaves of the trees have twelve kinds of fruit and are for the healing of the nations.

TREES ON EARTH

Did you know that the oldest living tree known in the world is found in the Ancient Bristlecone Pine Forest in the White Mountains of California? This tree is known as "Methuselah" and is 4,798 years old. It is as old as the pyramids of Egypt.

Do you wonder, as I do, how this tree was able to survive? In my research, I discovered some of the survival characteristics and strategies that helped this tree to survive. I found out this tree lived in a harsh environment of whipping winds, ice, fires and harsh drought. This tree benefited from being isolated with a lot of space between each tree. The tree put more energy into surviving than growing tall or big.

TREES AND PEOPLE GROW INDIVIDUALLY

The Bristlecone Pine Tree put the most energy into surviving instead of growing tall. For us to be able to survive spiritually, we must put most of our energy into habitually studying the Word of God and praying that God will reveal to us how to best put these precepts into our daily life now. We will then be fed daily on sustaining food that will help us to survive during the turbulent, dark, painful days of our life, and we will not wither and be blown away by the storms of life.

One verse speaks of sinners in the assembly of the righteous. No amount of sitting in a church pew will help us survive if we do not individually take the Bible Truths home and individually study privately with prayers and meditation. We must have a humble spirit and a contrite heart asking God for understanding as we read and then choose to put these truths into practice. If you are not already doing so, consider starting today building a habit of daily time with God.

Next, let's consider the concept that a tree is rooted. Like trees, Christians are rooted and built up in Christ. (Col. 2:7) The roots of a tree supply food for the tree. If people are in Christ, there is abundance of strength. The weakness arises when we allow our roots to wander from Christ into evil and sinful ground. Don't be like a willow tree. This tree will go after water and when the water is removed, it will die. Some Christians are like this. They are great Christians if everything is going their way. However, when trials come, and the good times disappear, they fade away and die. This happens because they were not fastened to our Beautiful Savior Jesus Christ.

A healthy tree grows and drinks from the river of life.

> *"Then the angel showed me the river of the water of life, bright as crystal, flowing from the throne of God and of the Lamb through the middle of the street of the city; also, on either side of the river, the tree of life with its twelve kinds of fruit, yielding its fruit each month. The leaves of the tree were for the healing of the nations." (Rev 22:1-2 ESV) Those that eat from this tree will live forever.*
>
> *Jesus said that those who hunger and thirst after righteousness will be filled. (Matt. 5:6) and he said ask, and it will be given to you; seek and you will find; knock and it will be opened to you. (Matt. 7:7)*
>
> Jesus gave a warning about trees and the fruit of diseased trees: *"a healthy tree cannot bear bad fruit, nor can a diseased tree bear good fruit. Every tree that does not bear good fruit is cut down and thrown into the fire. Thus, you will recognize them by their fruit."* (Matt. 7:18-20).

A beautiful story is told in John 4. Jesus interacted with a Samarian woman drawing water from a well. Jesus used this encounter to tell her about living water.

"Jesus said to her, everyone who drinks of this water will be thirsty again, but whoever drinks of the water that I will give him will never be thirsty again. The water that I will give him will become in him a spring of water welling up to eternal life." (John 4:13-14 ESV)

"All Scripture is breathed out by God and profitable for teaching for reproof, for correction, and for training in righteousness, that the man of God may be complete, equipped for every good work." (2 Tim. 3:16 ESV)

"Blessed is the man who trusts in the Lord, whose trust is the Lord. He is like a tree planted by water, that sends out its roots by the stream, and does not fear when heat comes, for its leaves remains green, and is not anxious in the year of drought, for it does not cease to bear fruit. The heart is deceitful above all things, and desperately sick; who can understand it? I the Lord search the heart and test the mind, to give every man according to his ways according to the fruit of his deeds." (Jer. 17:7-10 ESV)

We must have a humble spirit and a contrite heart asking God for understanding as we read and then put these truths into practice.

BOOKS

"Every day of my life was recorded in your book."
(Psalm. 139:16b NLT)

When my children were born, I kept a baby book on their progress. First handprints, first footprints, first words, and my excitement about everything they accomplished. As they grew, I stopped the baby book and started photo albums. Now, I have several closets full of boxes of pictures. When my grown children come to see me, we enjoy remembering many events of the past as we look at the pictures, laugh, and see how we have changed and wonder how it all happened.

I find it interesting that God keeps books of remembrance on all his children. Since He created us, He loves us and shows it by keeping a record of all that is going on in our life. God's book is hidden from us now. However, God's revealed Word to us today is in the Bible. I especially love Psalms.

> "You keep track of all of my sorrows. You have collected my tears in your bottle. You have recorded each one in your book." (Ps. 56:8 NLT)

God cares about our feelings as we journey through life. He records all our tears. He remembers our pain and suffering.

Jesus Christ experienced extreme feelings of pain and suffering on the cross before he died and was resurrected. After He was resurrected, He gave us, as believers, the opportunity to experience the power of the Holy Spirit to help, guide and comfort us in our painful experiences.

Christ reaches down in our darkness and opens a curtain for us. We are blessed by a viewing of God's glorious light of Christ. In His beauty, he tenderly clasps our hand and lifts us up from the depths of despair.

When Stephen was stoned to death, Jesus stood (Acts 7:56-58). Recorded stories are important to God. He wrote the Ten Commandments on tablets of stone (Ex. 20:1-21) and worked with Moses to record the first five books of the Bible: Genesis, Exodus, Leviticus, Numbers and Deuteronomy.

God wanted the apostles to remember, and therefore Jesus took Peter, James and John to a high mountain. They were alone with Jesus and were able to see His earthly body transfigured into a dazzling, heavenly body. Peter, James and John also saw Moses and Elijah and heard their conversations. The three were stunned and wanted to know what it meant.

God wanted these special apostles to see their God-given place in the history of the earth. He wanted them to powerfully see that God gives us life after our physical death. Everyone has a purpose in the big picture. Moses represented the Law. Elijah represented the prophets. Jesus Christ represented God in a human body—showing the character of God the Father and the life-giving power of the Holy Spirit. (Mark 9:2-12) Jesus prophesied his death. (Mark 13:5-37) Jesus wants us to continually remember his death, burial and resurrection (Luke 22:14-20).

What is the Good News? The Apostle Paul used the Law of Moses and the books of the prophets to persuade about Jesus Christ (Acts 28:23). Paul used the transfiguration scene to help see the big picture (Mark 9:2-12).

It has been interesting to me to read about Moses death in Deuteronomy 34. The Lord buried him. In Jude verses 8–16, we read that Satan wanted the body of Moses. The mightiest angel, Michael, did not dare accuse the devil of blasphemy, but simply said, "The Lord rebuke you." (Jude verse 9)

Elijah also had an interesting story. He was a prophet during the reigns of King Ahab of Israel and King Jehoshaphat of Judah. After King Ahab died, King Ahaziah began to reign. Elijah did not die. God carried Elijah in a chariot of fire drawn by horses of fire in a whirlwind (2 Kings 1:1-18 to 2 Kings 2:1-15).

The story of Jesus' resurrection is beautifully told by him to the Apostle Thomas. "Put your finger here and look at my hands. Put your hand into the wound in my side. Don't be faithless any longer. Believe! Jesus ends with "You believe me because you have seen me. Blessed are those who believe without seeing me" (John 20:29 NLT)

John ends telling us the purpose for his book. "The disciples saw Jesus do many other miraculous signs in addition to the ones recorded in this book. But these are written so that you may continue to believe that Jesus is the Messiah, the Son of God, and that by believing in him you will have life by the power of his name." (John 20:30-31) NLT

The Word of God is alive. God reveals many great promises to us in His Word (Heb. 4:1-16). After promising rest for God's people in verses 1 – 11, he tells us God's Word is alive and powerful in verse 12.

He continues to explain how Christ is our High Priest and tells of our amazing privilege of prayer. Christ intercedes for us with God, the Father.

"So then, since we have a great High Priest who has entered heaven, Jesus the Son of God, let us hold firmly to what we believe. This High Priest of ours understands our weaknesses, for he faced all of the same testing we do, yet he did not sin. So, let us come boldly to the throne of our gracious God. There we will receive his mercy, and we will find grace to help us when we need it most."(Heb. 4:14-16 NLT)

"Every high priest is a man chosen to represent other people in their dealings with God. He presents their gifts to God and offers sacrifices for their sins. And he is able to deal gently with ignorant and wayward people because he himself is subject to the same weaknesses. That is why he must offer sacrifices for his own sins as well as theirs.

And no one can become a high priest simply because he wants such an honor. He must be called by God for this work, just as Aaron was. That is why Christ did not honor himself by assuming he could become High Priest. No, he was chosen by God, who said to him, 'You are my Son. Today I have become your Father.' And in another passage God said to him, 'You are a priest forever in the order of Melchizedek.'" (Heb. 5:1-6) NLT

God also keeps a Book of Life to record our acts of service (Phil. 4:3). Only those whose names are written in the Lamb's Book of Life will be allowed in Heaven with Christ (Rev 20:12; 21:27). All of these scriptures show that God knows every secret part of our life, thoughts, words and actions. This is a great comfort to those who worship God and obey Him, but it is terrifying to those who choose to do evil and deliberately rebel against God and do not honor or respect His Name—The Great IAM.

Instead of checking out the national news and getting caught up in the drama, stop, ask God to clear your mind and focus on the precious treasures of the moments in your now. Remember that God gave you this moment for a special purpose.

Grab your dusty Bible. Open it up. Ask God to direct your thoughts in this present moment. Close your eyes. Take a deep breath. Wait. See what happens.

"A voice said, 'Shout!' I asked, 'What should I shout?' Shout that people are like the grass. Their beauty fades as quickly as the flowers in a field. The grass withers and the flowers fade beneath the breath of the Lord. And so it is with people. The grass withers and the flowers fade, but the word of our God stands forever" (Isa. 40: 6-8) NLT.

THE WAY OF PEACE

Stop
Ask God to clear your mind.

Sit still
Take a deep Breath

Saturate
Your mind With God's Word.

See
The Big Picture

Seek
God's Will

Stand
Up with Courage

Sing songs
With joy and a thankful heart.

REFLECTIONS

1. Read Psalm 139:13-16.

2. Pray that God will give you understanding.

3. Spend time reflecting about your entire life: your parents; your culture; your age; your gender; personality; natural abilities; and weaknesses. Ask God to show you the plan that He has for your life.

4. Keep a prayer journal of all these thoughts. Record any new circumstances that unfold. Then, ask God to show you His plan for your life.

5. God always answers by pointing us to His Word. Then, as we embrace His Word, a new life story unfolds! Scripture always interprets Scripture.

6. As you continue this pattern, God will soon show you the power of your story. You will find the joy of sharing your story with others.

7. God's Omnipotence will be revealed to you. The Trinitarian Godhead: The Father, the Son Jesus Christ and the Holy Spirit will empower you to become the person he intended before you were born.

CHAPTER 7
Response To God's Greatness & Grace

How precious are your thoughts about me, O God. They cannot be numbered! I can't even count them; they outnumber the grains of sand! And when I wake up you are still with me!
—Psalm 139:17-18 NLT

O Lord my God. You have performed many wonders for us. Your plans for us are too numerous to list. You have no equal. If I tried to recite all your wonderful deeds, I would never come to the end of them.

—Psalm 40:5 NLT

The following is an example of how one godly man responded to God's greatness and grace.

STEPHEN

Stephen was a godly man and a disciple of Jesus Christ. He was chosen to spend his time with the daily distribution of food to the poor widows in the community. He was chosen because he was well-respected and full of the Holy Spirit and wisdom. Lying witnesses caused him to be arrested. The following Scripture tells of Stephen's address to the Council.

Then the high priest asked Stephen, "Are these accusations true?"

This was Stephen's reply: Brothers and fathers, listen to me. Our glorious God appeared to our ancestor Abraham in Mesopotamia before he settled in Haran. God told him, 'Leave your native land and your relatives, and come into the land that I will show you.' So Abraham left the land of the Chaldeans and lived in Haran until his father died. Then God brought him here to the land where you now live.

But God gave him no inheritance here, not even one square foot of land. God did promise, however, that eventually the whole land would belong to Abraham and his descendants—even though he had no children yet. God also told him that his descendants would live in a foreign land, where they would be oppressed as slaves for 400 years. 'But I will punish the nation that enslaves them,' God said, 'and in the end they will come out and worship me here in this place.'

God also gave Abraham the covenant of circumcision at that time. So when Abraham became the father of Isaac, he circumcised him on the eighth day. And the practice was continued when Isaac became the father of Jacob, and when Jacob became the father of the twelve patriarchs of the Israelite nation.

These patriarchs were jealous of their brother Joseph, and they sold him to be a slave in Egypt. But God was with him and rescued him from all his troubles. And God gave him favor before Pharaoh, king of Egypt. God also gave Joseph unusual wisdom, so that Pharaoh appointed him governor over all of Egypt and put him in charge of the palace.

But a famine came upon Egypt and Canaan. There was great misery, and our ancestors ran out of food. Jacob heard that there was still grain in Egypt, so he sent his sons—our ancestors—to buy some. The second time they went, Joseph revealed his identity to his brothers, and they were introduced to Pharaoh. Then Joseph sent for his father, Jacob, and all his relatives to come to Egypt, seventy-five persons in all. So.

Jacob went to Egypt. He died there, as did our ancestors. Their bodies were taken to Shechem and buried in the tomb Abraham had bought for a certain price from Hamor's sons in Shechem.

As the time drew near when God would fulfill his promise to Abraham, the number of our people in Egypt greatly increased. But then a new king came to the throne of Egypt who knew nothing about Joseph. This king exploited our people and oppressed them, forcing parents to abandon their newborn babies so they would die.

At that time Moses was born—a beautiful child in God's eyes. His parents cared for him at home for three months. When they had to abandon him, Pharaoh's daughter adopted him and raised him as her own son. Moses was taught all the wisdom of the Egyptians, and he was powerful in both speech and action.

One day when Moses was forty years old, he decided to visit his relatives, the people of Israel. He saw an Egyptian mistreating an Israelite. So Moses came to the man's defense and avenged him, killing the Egyptian. Moses assumed his fellow Israelites would realize that God had sent him to rescue them, but they didn't.

The next day he visited them again and saw two men of Israel fighting. He tried to be a peacemaker. 'Men,' he said, 'you are brothers. Why are you fighting each other?'

But the man in the wrong pushed Moses aside. 'Who made you a ruler and judge over us?' he asked. 'Are you going to kill me as you killed that Egyptian yesterday?' When Moses heard that, he fled the country and lived as a foreigner in the land of Midian. There his two sons were born.

Forty years later, in the desert near Mount Sinai, an angel appeared to Moses in the flame of a burning bush. When Moses saw it, he was amazed at the sight. As he went to take a closer look, the voice of the Lord called out to him, 'I am the God of your ancestors—the God of Abraham, Isaac, and Jacob.' Moses shook with terror and did not dare to look.

Then the Lord said to him, 'Take off your sandals, for you are standing on holy ground. I have certainly seen the oppression of my people in Egypt. I have heard their groans and have come down to rescue them. Now go, for I am sending you back to Egypt.'

So God sent back the same man his people had previously rejected when they demanded, 'Who made you a ruler and judge over us?' Through the angel who appeared to him in the burning bush, God sent Moses to be their ruler and savior. And by means of many wonders and miraculous signs, he led them out of Egypt, through the Red Sea, and through the wilderness for forty years.

Moses himself told the people of Israel, 'God will raise up for you a Prophet like me from among your own people.' Moses was with our ancestors, the assembly of God's people in the wilderness, when the angel spoke to him at Mount Sinai. And there Moses received life-giving words to pass on to us.

But our ancestors refused to listen to Moses. They rejected him and wanted to return to Egypt. They told Aaron, 'Make us some gods who can lead us, for we don't know what has become of this Moses, who brought us out of Egypt.' So they made an idol shaped like a calf, and they sacrificed to it and celebrated over this thing they had made. Then God turned away from them and abandoned them to serve the stars of heaven as their gods! In the book of the prophets it is written,

'Was it to me you were bringing sacrifices and offerings during those forty years in the wilderness, Israel? No, you carried your pagan gods—the shrine of Molech, the star of your god Rephan, and the images you made to worship them.

So I will send you into exile as far away as Babylon.

Our ancestors carried the Tabernacle with them through the wilderness. It was constructed according to the plan God had shown to Moses. Years later, when Joshua led our ancestors in battle against the nations that God drove out of this land, the Tabernacle was taken with them into their new territory. And it stayed there until the time of King David.

David found favor with God and asked for the privilege of building a permanent Temple for the God of Jacob. But it was Solomon who actually built it. However, the Most High doesn't live in temples made by human hands. As the prophet says,

'Heaven is my throne, and the earth is my footstool.

Could you build me a temple as good as that?' asks the Lord.

'Could you build me such a resting place?

Didn't my hands make both heaven and earth?'

You stubborn people! You are heathen at heart and deaf to the truth. Must you forever resist the Holy Spirit? That's what your ancestors did, and so do you! Name one prophet your ancestors didn't persecute! They even killed the ones who predicted the coming of the Righteous One—the Messiah whom you betrayed and murdered. You deliberately disobeyed God's law, even though you received it from the hands of angels."

The Jewish leaders were infuriated by Stephen's accusation, and they shook their fists at him in rage. But Stephen, full of the Holy Spirit, gazed steadily into heaven and saw the glory of God, and he saw Jesus standing in the place of honor at God's right hand. And he told them, "Look, I see the heavens opened and the Son of Man standing in the place of honor at God's right hand!"

Then they put their hands over their ears and began shouting. They rushed at him and dragged him out of the city and began to stone him. His accusers took off their coats and laid them at the feet of a young man named Saul.

As they stoned him, Stephen prayed, 'Lord Jesus, receive my spirit." (Acts 7:1-59 NLT)

DISCOVERING MY ANCESTOR PARSON HIRAM MILO FRAKES

Just as archeologists make great discoveries about our past, we too, find that our lives are built upon the shoulders of all humanity that have gone on before us, and some day our children, grandchildren and great-grandchildren will build their lives on what we have done. They will see our mistakes, sins, challenges, and see how we have decided to face them. Did we act courageously or cowardly, wise or foolish, good or evil, loving or hateful, humble or proud, forgiving or unforgiving, unifying or distrustful?

What kind of a foundation are you building for those who will follow after you are in the tomb, which is the common destiny of all of humankind?

When we rebel against our earthly family, our parents, our background, we are rebelling against God who created us at this time in history for a unique purpose that only we can fulfill. Have you taken the time—the God-given time—to look at your big picture? Have you prayerfully asked God to reveal to you the path He would like you to follow? His answer will always come. However, God's message will always agree with the context of the entire Bible.

In one of my Bible studies, I surveyed the Old and New Testament to discover themes. I was surprised to find the importance God placed on lineage. So, after pondering this, I wondered about my own heritage. What is God expecting me to do? I prayed. God answered my prayer.

At just the right time, during a very dark period in my life, while I was discouraged amid the insecurity of living in twenty-seven different homes and having fifteen different jobs, I discovered that my beloved Mother was dying of cancer. We lived in Winston-Salem, North Carolina at this time, and my parents lived in San Diego, California.

During Mother's long illness, I wanted desperately to know more about my ancestors. When we made our final trip to California, as I was talking to Daddy in their little apartment, he suddenly put a large box in my lap.

"Do you want this box?" he asked.

I carefully peeked inside the box and discovered a twenty-five-year-old research project that my great-aunt Etta Logan had recorded from her discoveries about my ancestors on my mother's side of the family.

I cried. Gave my Daddy a big hug and joined the others gathering in their little apartment next door to the church building.

Later, while back in Winston-Salem, I was able to inspect all the research. It was so surprising to discover the story of my great-great-great grandfather, Asa Frakes.

I told his story in my book, *God's House! Beautiful! Let's Go!* Here is a summary of the story of his life.

Asa Frakes was born in Nelson County Kentucky April 10, 1803. His family moved to Prairie Creek, Indiana. He married Rebecca Dickinson February 19, 1824 and they had ten children. They lived on a farm. He operated a grocery store and preached for the Little Flock Baptist Church in Prairie Creek, Indiana for thirty-eight years until his death December 8, 1873. When we lived in Greensboro, North Carolina, the step-daughter of my great-aunt Etta Logan, located our address and drove from Florida to give me the cane that belonged to Asa Frakes.

As I inspected another large packet of papers, I discovered the story of Hiram Milo Frakes. With the known information found in the packet and elsewhere, I think he must have been Asa Frakes great-nephew from the line of Asa's older brother William. Little by little, I kept researching all this information.

To my surprise I discovered a book had been written about the life of Hiram Frakes by Lee Fisher, called *Fire in the Hills.* Henderson Settlement has graciously given me permission to include this condensed story from this book.

"What God Hath Wrought"
(A sign outside the Post Office in Frakes, Kentucky)

Where is Frakes, Kentucky? It is just north of the Tennessee State Line to the South and a few miles from the Virginia State Line toward the east. The area was first settled in the 1850's by poor immigrants from Scotland and Ireland. In the early days the chief means of making a living was farming, mining and moonshining. This area was nicknamed "South America" because of its remote inaccessibility.

The Light

Lord, You light my lamp; my God illuminates my darkness.
—Psalm 18:28 (HCSB)

In 1925 Parson Hiram Frakes entered a packed courtroom in Pineville, Kentucky, to attend a murder trial. Throughout the three years in hill country, Hiram had been no stranger to courtroom proceedings. As secretary for the local church's social service work he had come to grips with every kind of human problem—from petty theft to murder. Like his Master he had a compassion for the poor, the brokenhearted, and those held captives by sin. He was drawn like a magnet to scenes of human suffering. It must have been so, for he didn't know the exact reason he tiptoed into that courtroom on that cold February day. He only knew that the judge, one of his church members, was presiding over a murder hearing in the county courtroom and he felt a strong urge to be there.

Seated in the front rows of the courtroom were clusters of gloomy-faced mountaineers—tall and gaunt and sullen. In ominous silence they stared defiantly back at the bench, their hands tucked into overall suspenders and their bearded jowls chewing in rhythmic unison on tobacco cuds. For two days now they had sat thus, motionless as statues, mum as mutes. A particularly vicious feud had flared up in their section, about twenty miles away. They had been summoned as witnesses. With the help of their testimony the court had hoped to fix blame for some of the killings that had taken place. A hope, it developed, as optimistic as it was vain. Small wonder then that the judge's patience had burst its seams.

As Frakes entered the courtroom, he noted that the presiding judge was unusually disturbed, and his face was flushed from anger.

"All right!" the judge shouted, "you won't talk. You won't brand the criminals. You won't help establish law and order in your community, so your children can have a decent chance at life. I suggest you all go back home to your South America and shoot and maim and murder until you're all killed off. Then we will come in and establish a civil government. Court's adjourned!"

The judge banged his gavel with a vengeance, disgust written all over his face. He was tired of trying to help these people who seemed to have no desire to help themselves.

The silent men of the mountains shuffled to their feet slowly and, almost insolently, walked from the courtroom. As the last one passed through the door, the judge turned to see Hiram Frakes beside him.

"Howdy, parson," he said. "Sorry you caught me backsliding with such an un-sanctified temper, but those…"

"I've been hearing a lot about that South America clan lately, Judge. Everybody says it's the worst spot in the United States for moonshining and feuding," Frakes interrupted.

"In the world, you mean," The judge amended. "There's not an adult male in the whole ten square miles out there who isn't engaged in making illicit liquor, and more people have been killed in feuds out there than in all the rest of Kentucky put together."

The judge wiped the sweat from his forehead and continued. "Two-thirds of all the cases before this court come from South America, and we get a conviction only once in a blue moon."

Parson Frakes and the mountaineer started up the twisting mountain trail. Thin wisps of fog clustered above the little coves, and smoke ascended from the tiny cabins perched on the sides of the steep slope.

As they came to the summit, Frakes couldn't believe his eyes. Below him stretched one of the greenest and fairest valleys he had even seen. It was like some fabled Brigadoon in the Scottish Highlands. There were groves and fields and meadows. He shut his eyes briefly. He could envision a school building with happy children running in and out and a steepled church with worshippers entering a spotless sanctuary, and the end of violence and feuding which had beleaguered these bloody hills for years.

A prayer crossed his lips: "O God, I don't know how you're going to do it, but give this valley to me, and I'll nourish it like a Garden of Eden."

The Darkness

Rescue those being taken off to death and save those stumbling toward slaughter. —*Proverbs 24:11 (HCSB)*

But when the goodness and love for man appeared from God our Savior, He saved us—not by works of righteousness that we had done, but according to His mercy, through the washing of regeneration and renewal by the Holy Spirit.
          —*Titus 3:4-5 (HCSB)*

Bill Henderson was known throughout those mountains as the "King of the Moonshiners." When Frakes met Henderson, he knew he must handle the man carefully. His guide had told him that Bill counted his misdemeanors against the law by notches on his gun—and those notches numbered thirteen! Just so, there were thirteen indictments lodged against him at the courthouse in Pineville. He was the honorary head of a feuding clan, revered by his clansmen, feared by his enemies, and sought constantly by the police. His trusty shooting iron stood between him and apprehension by the law.

Frakes decided to approach Bill Henderson just as he had the others, in honesty and openness. He told him of his dream for the valley and challenged him for the sake of his wife and children to be a part of it. Bill Henderson's land was the most valuable land in the entire area. Bill listened intently as Frakes described Laurel Creek as it could be, and when Frakes finished, Bill eyed him silently for a long time. Then he stood up, shoved his hands in the pockets of his overalls, threw back his shoulders, and said, "Preacher, I don't do things halfway. When I'm sold on something, I'm sold all the way. I'll just give you the whole sixty-eight acres."

Frakes couldn't believe his ears. Shocked, because he'd heard even in Pineville about the meanness of Bill Henderson, he asked for confirmation. "Do you mean you're going to give all the land you own?"

"Yep, that's what I mean," Bill assured him. He went on, "I know my days are numbered, preacher. The law is after me hard; and if, when they git me, you'll take care of my kids, the land is yours."

The parson's years at Laurel Fork were like the weather the good Lord gives, a mixture of clouds and sunshine, of rain and fair weather. A victory would be gained, only to be followed by discouraging incident.

THE CONFLICT

For the word of God is living and effective and sharper than any two-edged sword, penetrating as far as to divide soul, spirit, joints and marrow, it is a judge of the ideas and thoughts of the heart. No creature is hidden from Him, but all things are naked and exposed to the eyes of Him to whom we must give an account.

—Hebrews 4:12-13 (HCSB)

Christ said: "They that take the sword shall perish with the sword" (Matt. 26:52). That statement could be paraphrased to say: "He that takes a gun shall perish with a gun," and the mountain people were aware of this law. The wailing of a widow en route to the cemetery to bury her husband who had been shot was a common sound in these hills. Death stalked the mountain trails, and a somber realization rested on every mountain man that he might be the next to die.

Bill Henderson died as he had lived—by a gun! His gun with its thirteen notches was not even used in self-defense. Since Bill was a changed man, there is considerable doubt that he would have used it if he could have.

The last Sunday of Bill's life on earth he had given a Christian testimony at the church service at Henderson Settlement. Stepping to the front of the little chapel with faltering words he said, "Hit's borne in on me like I ort to testify here and now fer hit might be my last chance. I'm feelin' proud to tell y'all at I've made my peace with Almighty God, and thar hain't nothing atween me an' my Lord."

They were prophetic, those words "Hit might be my last chance," for it was. But that testimony rang in the ears of those attending the service that night, and they knew that Bill Henderson was a changed man. This man who they all knew had killed thirteen men in his life had found a new forgiveness and God!

Three days later Bill Henderson took his last ride. Not erect in the saddle saying, "Howdy" to fellow mountain folk, as was his custom in life; but in death, with a haunting smile on his face as if he were saying,

"I've found peace at last." Now he was free of all the feuding, the hate, the rigors of mountain life at Laurel Fork.

Parson Frakes had lost a good friend; but right now, he had to face the fact that there might be friends and relatives of Bill's out for revenge. This had always been the unwritten code of the mountains. These next days could be crucial to Laurel Fork. With a heavy heart, he thought about slipping away into Pineville and turning the service for Bill over to the mountain preachers. It would have been the easy way, and he was very, very tired, as he had suffered a severe loss in Bill's death.

But Frakes was never one to run from divine duty. His temptation was tempered with the knowledge that the mountain folk have their ways and perhaps it would be best to let them pursue their ancient drama of death.

When he was first called to preach, the word of the Lord had come to him: "Preach the preaching I bid thee preach." But still came the recurring thought that perhaps the mountain preachers could handle this delicate situation better. As he sought guidance in the matter, the words of Scripture came to him. "Who knoweth but that thou art come to the kingdom for such a time as this?"

Out of his terrific inner struggle came this chastened answer to God, "You've helped me so far in these hills, and I know you'll lead me on." Putting an end to his soul's conflict, he added these submissive words, "I'll do what you want me to do."

The church was filled for Bill's funeral. After his own daughters along with the glee club from the Settlement school sang, "Jesus, lover of My Soul," Frakes stepped to the foot of Bill's coffin, took his small Testament from his pocket, and read slowly and impressively the third chapter of James.

Then with deep feeling he began to speak, "My friends, we are here to commit the body of William Henderson to the earth and his soul to God. We all know how swift his summons was. But we know too that he died with a prayer on his lips, and we are willing to stake our lives on God hearing that prayer. I am not here to pronounce a eulogy over this man, who was my friend. Yet I must mention the fact that repeatedly since this tragedy men have said to me: "Bill Henderson was a good neighbor. He had a kind heart."

"I shall never forget one Sunday morning at the Settlement when Bill saw his daughter Mabel at the piano for the first time. As he heard her play the hymns of the church, tears ran down his bronzed cheeks. He was unashamed of those tears, being the man he was. At the close of the service he said to me, "Parson, we're kind of an uncivilized lot, quarreling and fighting like we do; but my daughter Mabel here is gonna' be different. He seemed happy at the thought that one day things would change.

"But, my friends, it is not of the dead I would speak today, but of us who remain. What will be our reaction to this tragedy? Shall we choose revenge and blighting hate? Or shall we be brave enough and big enough in our souls to see the better way, the way that makes for peace? "Vengeance is mine, I will repay, saith the Lord."

Then fondling the little New Testament, he again quoted from James: *"The tongue is a fire, a world of iniquity.... It defileth the body and setteth on fire the course of nature and is set on fire of hell......It is an unruly evil, full of deadly poison."* He then said, *"Words are weapons that kill, and God is the only conqueror of our temper and our tongues."*

A few people squirmed nervously, realizing that even a preacher is not immune from mountain revenge, and they were astounded by Frakes's courage in trying to come to grips with the issue surrounding Bill Henderson's death.

The sobbing so common at a mountain funeral ceased. Under the stately, swaying hemlock God's message was going home, healing, strengthening, curing the hatreds of the hills.

Even Bill's own son-in-law Otis, who, according to his own words, was "hot with wrath inside," said, "I reckon now I can hold my peace."

That funeral sermon set the pace for the years ahead. Its truth will echo in the hearts of all those present for time to come. The Parson had dared to step out, as he had many times before, on the empty void, only to find the Solid Rock beneath.

Bill Henderson was dead. But his death occasioned a spiritual flame which still burns in those hills to this very day. "He being dead, yet speaketh."

Victory in Christ

Now since the children have flesh and blood in common, He also shared in these, so that through His death He might destroy the one holding the power of death—that is, the Devil—and free those who were held in slavery all their lives by the fear of death.

—Hebrews 2:14-15 (HCSB)

A news item on the front page of the *Middlesboro Daily News*, February 7, 1963.

The Rev. Hiram M. Frakes, 74 years old, founder of Henderson Settlement, now known as Frakes, Kentucky, leaves Bell County this week to end an era.

With nothing but courage and determination, Frakes took education, evangelism, and civilization to an area that had known much moonshining and senseless bloodshed. He built the Settlement from a one-room schoolhouse to its present 22 buildings and over 750 acres of land.

Frakes, for forty-one years, during the years from 1922 to 1963, had witnessed miracle after miracle. He had seen the people of Laurel Fork community shift from moonshining and hog-raising to church-going, school-attending, and respectability. He saw the first drop-reaper unloaded in the valley; the first scientifically planted apple orchard; the first field of wheat; the first clover field; the first cattle testing; the first modern houses; the first up-to-date school; the first boarding school; the first honor students; the first college graduates; the first Men's Brotherhood; the first 4-H Club; the first rural mail service; the first paved road to Laurel Fork community; the first airplane; the first machine shop; the first tractor; the first basketball team; the first planned revival; the first community celebrations; the first Laurel Fork Fair;

and the first full year without a murder in the community. Firsts, firsts, firsts! Frakes had seen all these and many more."

Perhaps the reason for these great accomplishments was that the Parson took the words of the Christ he served literally: "Seek ye first the kingdom of God, and all these things will be added unto you." They had been added in abundance.

Frakes never once dreamed, when he visited Washington with his quartette one year, that they would be received and commended by President Herbert Hoover as he met them in the White House garden and was full of praises for the work of Henderson Settlement.

In studying the lives of great Christians, one cannot overlook the fact that God seems more interested in men and women who would become tools in his hands than in men and women who would use him as a tool. Perhaps the Lord's strategy in using the ordinary to do the extraordinary is that he wants the world to know that it is not by might nor by power, but by my Spirit, saith the Lord.

(Condensed and used by permission from Fire in the Hills by Lee Fisher —The Story of Parson Frakes and the Henderson Settlement 2005 Frakes, Kentucky)

As I have tried to process all this research about my family history, I get cold chills. When I think about all the intricate circumstances that God has created to answer my prayer, I wonder what he wants me to gain by having this knowledge?

I marvel at the majesty and greatness of God and His interest in the little things that bother me. The contrast is mind boggling. I do not have the words to express my thanks for his grace, mercy, compassion and kindness to me!

The above excerpts from the book, *Fire in the Hills* by Lee Fisher only gives a glimpse of the power of this story. At one time Lee Fisher served as pastor, coach, and medical officer at Henderson Settlement and he has remained in touch with Hiram Frakes and the settlement throughout the years until Hiram Frakes died. In addition, Lee Fisher served on the Billy

Graham team and as personal assistant to Dr. Graham. You would be greatly inspired by reading the entire book.

As I moved my heritage discovery project along, other great stories have been given to me that I will share. The next story comes from my hometown of Terre Haute, Indiana.

A Journey of Forgiveness
The Personal Story of Eva Mozer Kor

The doors of the cattle car were yanked opened. Orders were barked at the passengers; 'Out, as soon as you can, out. Your belongings [sic] you leave there!'

After three days spent jammed into the car with about 90 other people and little food or water and no toilet facilities except for a pan, 10-year-old Eva Mozes Kor thought just getting off the train would be a relief.

Disoriented and tired, the passengers obeyed the orders, began exiting the cattle car and tried to get their bearings. What they got instead was their first look at Auschwitz, the Nazis' largest concentration camp, and a premonition of their fates.

For Kor, however, her first step onto the railroad platform was the beginning of an incredible journey to survival and, ultimately, forgiveness of those who persecuted and tortured her.

'The state of mind when we arrived was sheer shock,' Kor says of their arrival at the camp near Krakow, Poland. 'I don't think that anybody knew what on earth was happening to us. Just chaos, shock.'

But the SS was nothing if not efficient. After exiting the car, the passengers were quickly formed into lines— women and small children in one and men and older boys in another—and the 'selection' process soon began.

Fate, in the form of Dr. Josef Mengele, was to intervene for Kor and her twin sister, Miriam, at this point, however. 'As we stepped down from the cattle car, my mother grabbed my twin sister and me by the hand, hoping that as long as she could hold onto us that she could protect us.' Kor remembers.

As Kor stood on the crowded platform and looked around, she noticed her father and two older sisters were nowhere to be found. She never saw them again.

An SS man stopped near the Kors, 'Zwillenge?' he asked. Twins?

'My poor mother didn't know what to say,' Kor says. 'She asked if that was good and the SS man nodded yes. And my mother said yes. Another SS man was brought in immediately. My mother was pulled to the right and we were pulled to the left. I looked back to see, and I saw my mother's arms stretched out in despair toward us as she was pulled away. I never even got to say goodbye to her because this was the last time we saw her.'

As Kor and her sister were being taken away, the rest of the passengers from their train started filing past an SS doctor who pointed either to the left or right with his thumb to indicate their fate. Those sent to the left went to the gas chambers; the ones who went to the right became slave laborers.

Because they were twins, the Kor sisters were something special in the world of Auschwitz. They were highly sought after as human guinea pigs for Dr. Mengele's genetic experiments. Dr. Mengele was searching for the secret of heredity and believed that twins held the answer to some of them.

As a result, Dr. Mengele did a number of medical experiments at Auschwitz on twins, using one twin as a guinea pig and the other as an experimental control. He carried out twin-to-twin transfusions, stitched twins together, and castrated or sterilized twins. Many twins had limbs and organs removed in surgical procedures that were performed without anesthesia.

The latest arrivals on the platform had yielded sixteen sets of twins for Dr. Mengele, including the Kors. The twins were quickly taken into a large building in the camp where bleachers lined one side of the building and shower heads lined the other. The twin's clothes were taken, and they sat naked on the bleachers waiting showers.

After showering, their clothes were returned, and a large red cross painted on the back of them. Kor learned years later in a Holocaust course at Indiana State University that the red cross signified the wearer was part of medical experiments.

'It seemed really, like a nightmare,' Kor remembers years later. 'If I somehow just closed my eyes and opened them up, the whole thing would disappear. And I even tried it. But the things did not disappear.'

The twins next were given short haircuts. As twins, they could keep their hair; everyone else in the camp had their head shaved. Then they were tattooed with an identification number. Kor was now A7063. That was her new identity.

That night in the barracks, Eva and Miriam were unable to sleep and went to the latrine. 'When we entered the place, there on the filthy floor were the corpses of three children.' Kor says. 'Their bodies were naked and shriveled and their eyes were wide open.

'And this is when I, as a 10-year-old, realized that unless I did something, Mariam and I also would end up on that filthy latrine floor. And so, I made a silent pledge that I would do anything within my power to ensure that Miriam and I did not end up on that filthy latrine floor.' She adds.

Life in the camp quickly settled into a routine for the Kors. Summer, winter, rain, or shine—no matter—there was roll call every morning. After roll call, the children returned to the barracks for Dr. Mengele's daily inspection, which included counting the twins. 'He wanted to know how many guinea pigs he had' Kor explains.

After Dr. Mengele's visit, the twins had a cup of brownish liquid for breakfast, and then the medical experiments would begin. During the experiments, one of the twins would have both arms tied to restrict blood flow. Blood would be t taken from their left arm, while five injections were administered in their right arm.

One day, after the injections, Kor grew deathly ill with a high fever. 'The rumor in the camp was,' Kor says, 'that anyone taken to the hospital never came back.'

Despite efforts to hide her illness, she was eventually taken to the infirmary. 'Twice a week trucks would come, and these poor living dead were thrown onto the trucks like sacks of potatoes.' Kor says. 'They knew what their future was to be; their screams were horrifying.'

On her first morning in the hospital, a fever-ridden Kor overheard Dr. Mengele tell the other doctors she had two weeks to live.'I made a silent pledge that I will prove Dr. Mengele wrong. I will survive and be reunited with Miriam.'

In the hospital fading in and out of consciousness, hovering between life and death, she continued to tell herself, 'I must survive.' After two weeks, Eva's fever finally broke, and she returned to the twins' barracks where she found Miriam sick.

Years later, after they were both grown, the sisters found out the truth behind Dr. Mengele's experiments. If the subject twin died, the other twin was killed with an injection to the heart and a comparative autopsy was performed. It was the only way two people who had the same genetic makeup could be studied.

Through all the suffering, however, liberation remained the dream. One day in early 1945 after the Nazis had fled the camp, the dream came true.

It was the middle of the day when one of the women went to the front of the barracks. It was snowing heavily that day. The visibility was very poor. And she started yelling at the top of her voice. 'We are free! We are free!' When we all ran to the front of the barracks, I couldn't see anything. I looked to the right, looked to the left. I couldn't see anything just snow. Until finally, I could made out the faces of Red Army soldiers clad in white camouflage clothes from the top to the bottom. They were smiling. When we ran up to them, they have us hugs, chocolate and cookies. This was the first taste of freedom. And the first time since I arrived in Auschwitz that anyone treated us with humanity and kindness. That was liberation day.

It was January 27, 1945, to be exact, and Kor had kept her promise. She and Miriam had survived. They were lucky. Of the estimated 3,000 'Mengele twins,' only about 200 were still alive at the end of the war.

Eve and Miriam went on to live with an aunt and uncle before moving to the new country of Israel in 195-. After serving eight years in the Israeli army, Eva married Michael Kor, moved to the United States, began a career as a real estate agent in Terre Haute and raised two children, Alex, and Rina.

After her children were grown, she decided to attend Indiana State university, where, ironically, one of her first classes dealt with the Holocaust.

'I knew nothing about my academic abilities,' she explains. 'I was treading on sacred ground as far as I was concerned. And so, I thought I would take a class that at least I would be familiar with.'

On her first day of class she approached the professor, 'I sure hope, I pass your class,' she remembers telling him. 'It would be embarrassing to survive the real thing and flunk your class. 'I was very serious.' She took night classes to fit her work schedule, and in 1990, eleven years after she began, Kor earned a degree in vocational technical education at the age of 56. 'I had never ever graduated from anything in my life,' she declares. 'For me to be able to really accomplish it was very important.

'I think it was a good way of opening new horizons for me and teaching me how to focus on certain things. My children were very proud that I didn't give up until I graduated. But it was mostly, just for me. I wanted at least to be able to prove to the world that I am not only a survivor, but I can get an education also and use my brain,' she added.

Despite all the positive things that happened in her post-war life, Kor still couldn't shake the memories of her nine months at Auschwitz. In my mind as I was growing up, Auschwitz loomed as a big giant monster. Auschwitz is very big but was no longer a place that could hurt me. I desperately tried to understand how my parents disappeared from the face of the earth, my sisters, I tried to understand what happened to them. It's very difficult to try to understand it, because they just marched to the gas chamber and vanished. Even today, it is difficult to understand.'

Beginning in the mid -1990s, however events began taking shape that would lead her to come to terms with those unspeakable atrocities and to forgive those who perpetrated crimes against her, her family and her people.

In 1995, she received a call from a professor at Boston College asking her to speak before a group of doctors there. She agreed.

'And then he said to me the strangest thing,' Kor recalls. He said, 'Well, when you come to the conference, would you please bring with you a Nazi doctor? And I said, 'What? Where do you think I can find a Nazi doctor? Last time I looked in the Yellow Pages there weren't any advertising in there.' And he said, 'Well, think about it. Maybe you'll come up with an idea.' 'It was intriguing that somebody would even ask me such a question or come up with an idea, and I did think about it."

Kor contacted Dr. Hans Munch, an SS doctor who served at Auschwitz and whom she had seen on a television documentary about the Holocaust. While he declined to speak with her at Boston College, he agreed to meet with her in his home.

'I was very nervous,' Kor admits. 'What I knew about Nazi doctors was not making me very comfortable. But I was also very curious. What was it like to be a Nazi doctor in Auschwitz? I only knew what it was like to be a victim.'

Dr. Munch, however, was an atypical SS doctor. He had refused to make selections at Auschwitz and testimony from prisoners that he had treated them humanely and saved their lives won him an acquittal at a war crimes trial.

Kor said that Munch treated her with 'utmost respect', answering her questions about the operation of the Auschwitz gas chambers. He called Auschwitz the 'nightmare I live with.' 'Strange thing. Here you are, a doctor from Auschwitz, here I am, a survivor of Auschwitz and I like you and that is very strange to me.'

Months after the visit, to find a way to express her appreciation to Munch for his candor and respect, Kor struck upon the idea of a 'letter of forgiveness.'

In doing so, she realized she possessed the power to forgive. 'No one could give me that power and no one could take it away. Victims of every type of situation always feel hurt, angry, hopeless, helpless and powerless. And I discovered at the other end that I had tremendous powers. That really made me feel good inside.'

She took the letter to Susan Kaufman her English professor at Indiana State. Kor remembers the conversation. Kaufman said, 'So you're going to forgive Dr. Munch?' 'Yes, with just a little letter from me to him' she said. 'Well, what about Dr. Mengele?' I said. 'I haven't thought about that.' The thought that here I was, that little victim, a nobody under his feet, practically just a guinea pig whom he wouldn't give a minute's thought for my life or the loss of my life, yet I had the power to forgive the god of Auschwitz. That really made me feel good inside. I am not hurting anybody, so I might as well forgive Mengele.'

When she began preparations for her return to Auschwitz for the 50th observation of the liberation in 1995, she called Dr. Munch and ask him to come with her. She also asks him to sign a document confirming the existence of the gas chambers. Because he had been an SS doctor at Auschwitz, she believed his words would establish the reality of the gas chambers and the deaths there. He agreed to do so.

During ceremonies marking the 50th observation of the liberation of Auschwitz, at the remains of one of the camp's gas chambers, Eva Mozes Kor and Dr. Hans Munch signed documents. Hers was a document that forgave the Nazis; his was a document that verified the gas chambers had existed. Kor read both documents aloud.

'Looking up to the sky in Auschwitz, a very eerie place anyway, I felt that the millions of victims and my parents and my family were my witnesses.' Kor said of that occasion. 'And I immediately felt that a burden of pain was lifted from my shoulders, that I was no longer a victim of Auschwitz, that I was no longer a prisoner of my tragic past—that I was finally free.'

Mark Gibson is assistant director of
communications and marketing at ISTU
Indiana State University Magazine
Volume 8, Number 2
Fall 2005
Permission Letter Given July 7, 2016 Libby Roerig,
Director of Communications Editor, STATE Magazine
Indiana State University
104 Gillum Hall. Terre Haute, Indiana 47809

When I read the above story in the Indiana State University Magazine, I was devastated. My mind flashed on scenes from my childhood – fun times with our next door neighbors who would take my brother and me to the ice cream parlor and give us yummy Bratapfel apple dessert. Their last name was Gurman and they were German Jews. We were much too young to understand the Holocaust. My brother and I loved the Gurmans.

Jay Wertheimer, the owner of BDI Distributors, where I worked for nineteen years was also Jewish, and he would order Bratapfel from New York. My memory of the Gurman's always flashed when Fed-Ex delivered the Bratapfel and Jay would share with me. Sadly, Jay passed away in Florida in 2012 after suffering many years with a heart condition. I wondered if he'd had any family stories of that terrible Holocaust.

When I reflected on the theme of Ms. Kor's story, I believed God wanted me to see the importance and value of forgiveness. I pondered on Eva Mozes Kor's closing words, "And I immediately felt that a burden of pain was lifted from my shoulders, that I was no longer a victim of Auschwitz, that I was no longer a prisoner of my tragic past—that I was finally free."

As Sinclair Ferguson said, "When you have a superficial view of sin, you will have a superficial view of grace." When Satan's lies invade our thoughts, as his seeds of evil grow, we become unable to comprehend the wisdom that God outlines in the pages of the Bible. Prayers for our enemies heal us so that we can forgive ourselves and allow God to touch the hearts of people who have not experienced the love of God in their life. They are blind.

SINGLE WOMAN MISSIONARY

In 2013 one of my best friends, Lisa, shared her testimony with a co-worker who had been a Muslim. This young Muslim lady accepted Jesus Christ as her personal Savior. Later, quite unexpectedly my friend Lisa died. She had told this young Muslim convert that I would help her in her new Christian life. When I learned about this, I was overwhelmed with how to help her. I prayed.

Soon, I was invited to attend the Kathy Jolly Missionary Circle at the Sawnee Drive First Baptist Church in Cumming, Georgia. While at this meeting, I heard a single woman missionary speak. She told of how she'd spent sixteen years doing mission work in the Arabic-speaking Muslim Culture in North Africa, West Africa and in the Middle East. She requested I not reveal her name. Therefore, I will call her SWM. Below is her inspiring story:

SWM's experience has been mostly in Arabic-speaking Muslim Cultures:

- 5 short-term mission trips, dating from 2001 to 2017
- 8 years teaching in North Africa (2003-2011)
- 2 years in West Africa* (2011-2013)
- 1.5 years in the Middle East (2013-2015)

> *This was not an Arab-Muslim culture. Please note that while Arabic-speaking Muslims make up only about 1/4 of the Muslim-speaking world it is this population to which I am referring in my article. Apart from my two years in West Africa, most of my experience was based in North Africa and the Middle East, where there is the highest concentration of Muslims in the world (around 95%).*

When I made my first short-term trip to North Africa in May of 2001, I knew very little about the Muslim faith. My short-term team had studied together for several months in preparation for our trip, but this was the extent of my knowledge. Sixteen years later, my knowledge of that culture has grown immensely through my time living and working in a Muslim environment. At the same time, I would readily admit that my understanding still feels so small, given the depth and breadth that culture entails.

Though God has called me back to the United States for the foreseeable future, I will always treasure my time working and living in the Muslim countries to which He sent me earlier in life.

In contrast to the images and ideas in Western media, the majority of Muslims that I met were wonderful people of great hospitality. They were fun to be around, and I enjoyed my Muslim friends. I still think of them often.

Sadly, however, the overall climates of the cultures in which I lived were each permeated by fear, distrust, and sadness. The Muslim faith is built upon fear – fear of God and fear of those in (religious) power. Because the faith does not value honesty as a whole, members of the community – even of the same family – often do not trust in one another. Due to the lack of certainty about the end of life, all live wondering if they will have done enough to appease Allah upon death, leading to a terrible lack of hope and genuine sadness.

As a believer in this context, it was always my desire to live out my faith in such a way as to allow the peace, joy, and truth of the gospel to shine. Whenever given the opportunity, I took the chance to speak biblical truth. However, in a Muslim context one can "speak" volumes by their life even when words are not possible in a given scenario.

Having returned here to the U.S., I find myself quite frustrated at times by what seems to me to be two polarized views of Muslims and the Muslim world. It feels to me that there is the one group of people who can only see terrorists and barbarians when they look upon Muslims. On the other hand, there is a second group that would seem to think that Muslims are only wonderful, peaceable people with no fault. To me, both of these viewpoints are grossly simplistic and exaggerated.

I believe that if we in the west are to understand our Muslim neighbors we must first realize that not all Muslims are terrorists. In my experience, the vast majority of Muslims I have met are not so different from any other person in the world. They desire peace where they live, a good job to provide for their family, a better life for their children, and opportunities for joy and fun with friends and family. They despise the violence in the world and want no part of it. At the same time, it is foolish of us to believe that all Muslims feel this way. Certainly, within certain places, families, and cultures there is a radical adherence to the Muslim faith which leads its followers to commit horrible acts of violence against mankind – even other Muslims – in the name of Allah.

Thus, I believe that bridging the gap between Western and Muslim culture first requires us to adopt a learning posture. At first glance, we cannot possibly imagine the radically different way in which a Muslim views his/her world. From birth, children are indoctrinated into the faith as it permeates every aspect of the culture. When seeking to interact with a Muslim about matters of faith, it is imperative that we first understand their ideas of faith through listening carefully to what they have to say – both about their own Muslim faith as well as what they've been taught about our faith. Only by listening well can we begin to realize the enormous differences in our views of God.

There are far too many illustrations of this for me to mention them all but let me share just one. In our Western culture, our laws, behavior, and even our faith often center on the concept of guilt versus innocence. To a Muslim, this is of little importance in most matters. Muslim culture is built upon the idea of shame versus honor. A good Muslim does not make decisions based upon whether or not something is right or wrong. Rather, his main concern is whether his actions will bring about honor or shame. Even the Koran allows for Muslims to lie whenever needed. In one country that I lived, there was a well-known proverb that said, "It's better to lie than to lose your face."

This is just one small example of how different a Muslim's worldview is from our Christian perspective. Yet this simple concept alone plays out in millions of ways – from big to small. For example, one of the most frustrating scenarios for a westerner in a Muslim context is trying to build relationships through inviting Muslim friends over for tea or for a meal. In a Muslim culture, if someone invites you to his or her home and you turn him or her down, you have just shamed that person –an unspeakable offense. Instead, what is expected of you is to say "yes" even if you know that you are not/cannot come. Not showing up for this agreed upon meal or cup of coffee is not shameful at all. Many a western missionary has invited their Muslim friend over for a meal, prepared an elaborate spread of food, only to have the friend not show up...repeatedly.

In the face of such odds at trying to bridge the cultural gap, what are we to do? I believe that we must acknowledge that we'll never fully understand a culture so different from our own, all the while striving to do everything in our power to at least move in the right direction.

I still feel quite limited in my knowledge of Arab-Muslim culture. Yet, how very far I have moved toward understanding over the past sixteen years. Things that used to completely baffle me now make perfect sense – even if I disagree with them or believe them to be wrong. I still understand why they are done, given the cultural context. This understanding is very helpful when seeking to share Christ in a way that is relevant to a Muslim hearer. I feel strongly that it is the time I've spent listening to my Muslim friends which has helped me to make gains in this area.

Secondly, if we truly want to reach the Muslim world, I believe we must do something that is very difficult for us as westerners. We must slow down and invest time in relationships. Again, this is another way that the Muslim worldview is so different from ours. They do not view life – their faith, their career choices, their decision making, and so much more – from an individual point of view. For them, life is communal, and everything revolves around the family and community. Relationships dominate everything. In a Muslim culture, the right relationship can accomplish in five minutes what would otherwise literally take five months.

Therefore, as we reach out to our Muslim friends, we must remember that they expect us to invest time with them. They will not hear anything we have to say if we are not actively engaged in their lives. Admittedly, this can feel overwhelming at times. However, I feel we must do our best in this area because it is so important for them. Many a Muslim convert to Christianity has turned their back on their new faith because of the loneliness and isolation they have felt in their new faith community.

Finally, I would submit that we must remember that the most important strategy for reaching our Muslim friends is to be in constant prayer — prayer for us to be bold in our sharing of the gospel and prayer that our friends' hearts will be open when we do. Many examples are seen in the gospel times when Jesus did not follow the cultural norms of his day. He knew that the kingdom of God was for every culture and above every culture.

We will never do everything the right way in our dealings with those from another culture, but He can supernaturally intercede in the midst of our weakness. Even when we fail, He can bring victory. Navigating the cultural gap apart from Him is futile, as is any endeavor of faith without His abiding power. I have seen examples time and time again of moments when all my strategies were useless, but He came through, nonetheless.

In our time, God is giving dreams and visions to Muslims around the world as He reveals himself to them. Record numbers of Muslims are coming to Christ as they witness the current atrocities carried out by Muslims in the name of Allah. I firmly believe that if we, the church, are ready and willing, we can be a part of what He is doing in this age and see a great harvest!

While I was attending the First Baptist Church on Sawnee Drive in Cumming Georgia, I was privileged to hear the powerful testimony of Ozden Mansoori's belief in Jesus Christ as her personal Savior. She has graciously agreed to allow me to share her story

A POWERFUL TESTIMONY

I, Ozden Mansoori, was born into a restricted Muslim family. Even though my father was not so strict on wearing a hijab, I practiced every one of the required Islam pillars. My grandfather was a well-known wealthy man in his town. Not only was he known for his wealth, but also his dedicated life to Islam. He visited Mecca twice in his lifetime, and he would get up very early in the morning to do his morning prayer and to read the Qur'an at least an hour every day. He did this every day before opening his store in the marketplace. He had this same routine every day for his entire life. He would even close his shop during the prayer at noon to go to the mosque every day.

I have two brothers who are younger than me. Our parents sent us to our grandparent's town for three months every summer to spend time with them and to learn how to read the Qur'an and learn more about Islam. My grandfather would hire Imam, a tutor, to come to his house to teach us how to read and write Arabic so that we could understand the Qur'an better. He believed that wasn't enough, so he would also send us to the Mosque to read more and more. He would make competitions between my brothers and me to memorize verses and would pay us twenty-five cents for each verse we successfully recalled. I always felt obligated to pray five times a day to satisfy Allah, fast for thirty days, and to finish reading the Qur'an during the month of Ramadan every year.

In my college years, I continued doing what I used to do with no feeling for it but only through the obligation to my grandfather and Allah.

I met my husband Kevin Mansoori my first year of college. He was agnostic at the time, so I made him my excuse to stop practicing most of the Islam pillars except the prayers to satisfy my mother. After we got married and came over to America I stopped practicing Islam all together after a while. I believed in Allah and Mohammad still but showed no dedication.

Our son Ashkan was born in 1997. This was a miracle, yet we did not realize he was a miracle until later years. It all started when he was four years old. Ashkan would love to join his father in the morning when Kevin was shaving and talk to him, and practice shaving with him. One morning I was passing the bathroom when I heard his precious voice asking his father, "What is God?"

Kevin being agnostic, answered very simply "He is a creator, he owns the whole world." That was when Kevin and I realized we as parents had to give religious education to Ashkan. After a long discussion, we decided to raise Ashkan as a Muslim because he was born into a Muslim family. That meant that we needed to find a mosque for him to go to. This was between the years 2000-2001 when there weren't many mosques in Atlanta or even around Georgia except one in downtown Atlanta.

One Sunday we decided to visit and get the information about this mosque and what they offered.

We stepped into the building and immediately I felt overwhelmed, as if a dark presence covered my soul. Kevin felt the same. I still remember how fast we left that building. It was almost like something was pulling us away from the mosque.

Several weeks passed by when we started thinking again about Ashkan's religious education. This time our view was shifted to a totally different perspective. We agreed that since we were living in the USA and Ashkan was born a US Citizen, we would let him learn about Christian faith, so he won't grow up not being exposed to any religious education. That was when Kevin started searching for a Church.

We were suggested two choices by his friend and his boss: First Baptist Church in Woodstock and Holt Road Baptist Church. We choose his boss's church which made us drive a long way to the Marietta/Roswell area and pass several churches along the way. But the point for us was that, at least we would know one family at this church, so we wouldn't feel totally out of place. After a couple of visits, we decided to get Ashkan's religious education at the Holt Road Baptist church.

By 2001 we started attending their service pretty much every Sunday. Ashkan loved the church and loved the people. It was only one month into it when my husband Kevin had a change of heart which led to saving our marriage. Kevin's testimony is another story for another time, however, I do need to mention this, Kevin was so determined that we should have a Christian family and no matter how long it would take he will wait for me to get saved.

As we had previously talked about, I was born into a very religious family and was brought up as a religious person by my grandfather. I was okay accepting Jesus as a prophet but nothing greater. In my mind, I was a Muslim and believed it couldn't be possible to be welcomed into heaven just by faith and giving my life to Jesus. I came from a religion where good deeds were the steps to heaven and following Islam's pillars was the only way in. So, this idea of faith and the washing of my sins was a foreign idea to me.

Ten months passed after Kevin had accepted Jesus Christ into his life, and even I was witnessing the changes in his life, but I was still a Muslim. Kevin's last attempt for my salvation was for him to convince me to invite our pastor to our home, so he could have a talk with me. That wonderful pastor Jim probably thought he would be with us only for a couple of hours, but it wasn't until midnight before he left our home. My last words to him was, "Pastor Jim, I accept everything you have said, and I accept Jesus Christ but I'm Muslim."

Kevin was furious, but Pastor Jim stopped him immediately and made him promise he would not interfere or bother me any more on this subject. We slammed the doors and went to bed, but I couldn't sleep. There was a spiritual battle in my head that I couldn't stop, and I thought I was going crazy. All this spiritual warfare happening inside of me resulted in me lashing out in violence. I even punched Kevin so hard he woke up screaming. I know that these actions were not mine, but the result of the evil I was battling inside my heart and soul.

The next morning, my face was so swollen I couldn't recognize myself in a mirror and had to call in sick from work that day.

After Kevin and Ashkan left the house, I randomly opened the Bible. It was the book of Deuteronomy. I read only one verse, but it was so clearly the answer to my struggle. I read the book of Deuteronomy so many times that even till this day can't locate the verses I read. After a while I got

*up and decided to take a shower. During the shower, all I
remember was crying out so loud and remember thinking
that it couldn't be that easy to go to heaven.*

*I remembered my past and how I had to work so hard for
Allah's acceptance, so how could it be that easy with Christ?
Then suddenly an unexplainable quietness came, and I heard
this very soft-spoken voice telling me, "It's that easy."*

*At that moment, I got out of the shower and fell on my
knees and accepted Christ and invited him into my life. I got
up and called Kevin asking for the Pastor's phone number,
but I didn't tell him the reason until later that day. Pastor
and I spoke very briefly, and I remember him telling me that
I was the first person he knew to ever be saved through the
book of Deuteronomy.*

*Finding Jesus has changed me indefinitely by giving me
peace I never felt before, and to this day that remains true.
As a Muslim we were taught to "do" things to find eternal
happiness, but with Christ it is "done." He died on the cross
to wash away our sins, and by believing in him we shall not
die but have eternal life by his side.*

Ozden Mansoori

Kevin Mansoori, Ozden's husband, works as an evangelist to Muslim families in the Atlanta area. At my request, he wrote the following article, the goal of which is to reach a mutual understanding between Muslims and Christians:

BUILDING BRIDGES — NOT WALLS

The key to successfully reaching a Muslim family is by building a bridge of understanding and avoiding putting up any walls of judgment. We should acknowledge where their faith in Islam originates. For example, we must factor in the different cultures depending on what country they came from or what denomination they practice (Sunni, Shi'a, or Sufi). This willmake it much easier for both sides.

EFFECTIVE COMMUNICATION

To have effective communication depends mostly on the knowledge you possess on their culture; like their language, dialect, and interests.

Developing a Clear and Mutually Shared Definition of the Problem. The problem starts when we ignore the fact that we are all equal in the eyes of God. We are saved and will share the kingdom of God with all our brothers and sisters. They are lost but our prayers are that they will find their way one day through the power of our Lord Jesus Christ. When they feel and see our love and our likeness to them, then all problems will dissolve and the formation of love and trust through faith will be established.

BUILDING BRIDGES OF UNDERSTANDING

To construct a solid bridge of understanding, one must first develop trust and a good relationship with the person/family that you are praying will find salvation. Although it may take time, you can accomplish this by waiting until they show an interest in our faith, then by listening to their questions and truthfully showing that you care for them.

APPRECIATIVE THINKING

Serving our Lord should be desired and enjoyable. To reach someone who is an unbeliever, we must show them the grace and love that Christ showed for us.

STRUCTURED DIALOGUE

We must approach an unbeliever prepared for answering the questions they might have. With patience and self-control, God will work through us to save them.

CREATE CONNECTIONS

Creating a connection should be the first step in reaching an unbeliever. Nobody will share their life's story or their beliefs without knowing you and trusting you first. Talking to them daily even if it is over the phone or email and involve yourself in their lives somehow (sharing a meal or helping with problems they might be facing) makes a huge impact on how they come to see you as a person and as a Christian.

Tell Me How You See the Problems

The problem starts when a Muslim thinks we are just there to convert them. Although that is our end mission, we must show them that we care and love them, and that is the purpose we are interacting with them. Besides, it is our love that we have for our Lord and his children that bring us to want to share the Good News.

How Active Listening Would Move the Cycle in the Right Direction

Active listening shows the speaker that you are engaged in the conversation and shows that you are presenting your faith in a selfless way. If you just nod your head and grunt when they are speaking and opening to you, what is stopping them from giving you the attention you desire when it is your turn to speak. Respect must come from both sides to achieve any kind of progress.

Kevin and Ozden Mansoori, March 2018

REFLECTIONS

---

1. Read Psalm 139:17-18 and Psalm 40:5. Ask God to give you understanding.

2. Reflect now on who you are. Think about your parents. Where were you born? Who is in your family? Who are your grandparents? Were you an orphan? A foster child? Who took care of you?

3. As you reflect on who and where you are now, remember to interlace these facts with Psalm 139 and Psalm 40. Yes, God placed you here, now, for a special purpose that no one else can fill.

4. Does this mean that if you rebel and curse your background that you are rebelling against God? Research other Scriptures to also help in your search.

5. Read Gen. 37:1—Gen. 50: 1-27 and reflect on the life of Joseph.

6. What did Joseph do about his background? Did he accept it? Did he reject it and blame God? What did God do to bless Joseph? Did God bless Joseph so he could bless and forgive others?

7. Does that story tell us God blesses us where we are? Even in dark painful circumstances?

8. Read Psalm 11 and ask God to show you that He rules in every circumstance in our life. Reflect now where and when God is continuing to do that to you.

9. Do you need to forgive someone in your life to release you from the bitter, dark prison of unforgiveness?

10. Write your thoughts in a prayer journal today.

PART FOUR
God's Holiness

The Scriptural meaning of the term Holy as described by R. C. Sproul, means first that it is separate, in a class by itself, or a cut above something. It is unique with no rivals or competition. God is so far above and beyond us that He seems totally foreign to us.

Scriptures for further study include: 1 Sam. 2:2; Ps. 86:8-10; 99:1-3; Is. 6:3-5; 40:25; 57:15; Hosea 11:13a.

To be holy is to be morally pure. When things are made holy, when they are consecrated, they are set apart unto purity. For God to be holy is for Him to be holy in relation to every aspect of His nature and character. The holiness of God is a matter of great importance to every living soul.

Google search www.bible.org R C Sproul 1/20/18

CHAPTER 8
Mysteries and Secrets

O God, if only you would destroy the wicked! Get out of my life, you murderers! They blaspheme you, your enemies misuse your name. O Lord, shouldn't I hate those who hate you? Shouldn't I despise those who oppose you? Yes, I hate them with total hatred for your enemies are my enemies.
—Psalm 139:19-22 NLT

The secret things belong to the Lord our God, but the things that are revealed belong to us and to our children forever, that we may do all the words of this law.
—Deuteronomy 29:29 ESV

For as long as I can remember I have spent hours reading. Some of the books that interested me as a child were mystery series. I would work hard for my parents so I could earn my weekly allowance to purchase one more book. Some of my collections were the Judy Bolton and Nancy Drew Mystery Series. I enjoyed the excitement of trying to discover the clues that led to solving the mystery. It was natural in my Bible studies to enjoy the excitement of discovering new Bible treasures. Since I believe the Bible is its own best interpreter, I rely heavily on in-depth Bible Studies. In my recent secret times with God, I found a new Bible treasure I have been trying to solve. It is the Scripture below.

Jane Ann Derr

The War in Heaven

> *Then there was a war in heaven. Michael and his angels
> fought against the dragon, and his angels. And the dragon lost
> the battle, and he and his angels were forced out of heaven.
> This great dragon—the ancient serpent called the devil or
> Satan the one deceiving the whole world—was thrown down
> to the earth with all his angels. Then I heard a loud voice
> shouting across the heavens, "It has come at last—salvation
> and power and the Kingdom of our God, and the authority of
> his Christ. For the accuser of our brothers and sisters has been
> thrown down to earth—the one who accuses them before our
> God day and night. And they have defeated him by the blood
> of the Lamb and by their testimony. And they did not love
> their lives so much that they were afraid to die. Therefore,
> rejoice, O heavens! And you who live in the heavens, rejoice!
> But terror will come on the earth and sea, for the devil
> has come down to you in great anger knowing that he has
> little time. . . .And the dragon was angry at the woman
> and declared war against the rest of her children—all who
> keep God's commandments and maintain their testimony for
> Jesus" (Rev. 12:7-12 & 17 NLT).*

Do war stories fascinate you? War means engaging in conflicts and defining the characters who are opposed to each other, and the purpose of the conflict. To best understand this passage of Scripture, we must search the Bible to see what God has revealed to us.

The Cast of Characters

Who is Michael?

> *I say this because some ungodly people have wormed their way
> into your churches, saying that God's marvelous grace allows
> us to live immoral lives. The condemnation of such people
> was recorded long ago for they have denied our only Master
> and Lord Jesus Christ. So I want to remind you, though you*

already know these things that Jesus first rescued the nation of Israel from Egypt, but later destroyed those who did not remain faithful. And, I remind you of the angels who did not stay within the limits of authority God gave them but left the place where they belonged. God has kept them securely chained in prisons of darkness waiting for the great day of judgment, and don't forget Sodom and Gomorrah and their perversion. Those cities were destroyed by fire and serve as a warning of the eternal fire of God's judgment. In the same way, these people--who claim authority from their dreams— live immoral lives, defy authority and scoff at supernatural beings. But even Michael, one of the mightiest of the angels, did not dare accuse the devil of blasphemy, but simply said, The Lord rebuke you! (This took place when Michael was arguing with the devil about Moses' body). But these people scoff at things they do not understand (Jude 4-10, NLT).

One of Michael's responsibilities is to guard God's community of believers. "God's angel sets up a circle of protection around us while we pray" (Ps. 34:7, MSG).

In the third year of the reign of King Cyrus of Persia, Daniel (also known as Belteshazzar) had another vision. He understood that the vision concerned events certain to happen in the future—times of great war and great hardship. When this vision came to me, I, Daniel, had been mourning for three whole weeks. All that time I had eaten no rich food. No meat or wine crossed my lips, and I used no fragrant lotions until three weeks had passed. On April 23, (Hebrew on the twenty-fourth day of the first month, of the ancient Hebrew lunar calendar. This date in the book of Daniel can be cross-checked with dates in surviving Persian records and can be related accurately to our modern calendar. This event occurred in April 23 536 BC) *as I was standing on the bank of the great Tigris River, I looked up and saw a man dressed in linen clothing, with a belt of pure gold around his waist. His body looked like a precious gem. His face flashed like lightning, and his eyes flamed like torches. His arms and feet shone like polished bronze, and his voice roared like a vast multitude of people.*

Only I, Daniel, saw this vision. The men with me saw nothing, but they were suddenly terrified and ran away to hide. So I was left there all alone to see this amazing vision. My strength left me, my face grew deathly pale, and I felt very weak. Then I heard the man speak, and when I heard the sound of his voice, I fainted and lay there with my face to the ground.

Just then a hand touched me, still trembling, to my hands and knees. And the man said to me: Daniel, you are very precious to God, so listen carefully to what I have to say to you. Stand up, for I have been sent to you. When he said this to me, I stood up still trembling.

Then he said, Don't be afraid, Daniel. Since the first day you began to pray for understanding and to humble yourself before your God, your request has been heard in heaven. I have come to answer your prayer. But for twenty-one days the spirit prince of the kingdom of Persia blocked my way. Then Michael, one of the archangels came to help me, and I left him there with the spirit prince of the kingdom of Persia. Now I am here to explain what will happen to your people in the future, for this vision concerns a time yet to come.

While he was speaking to me, I looked down at the ground unable to say a word. Then the one who looked like a man touched my lips and I opened my mouth and began to speak. I said to the one standing in front of me, 'I am filled with anguish because of the vision I have seen, my lord, and I am very weak. How can someone like me, your servant, talk to you, my lord? My strength is gone, and I can hardly breathe.'

Then the one who looked like a man touched me again, and I felt my strength returning. 'Don't be afraid,' he said, 'for you are very precious to God. Peace! Be encouraged! Be strong!'

As he spoke these words to me, I suddenly felt stronger and said to him, 'Please speak to me, my lord, for you have strengthened me.'

He replied, 'Do you know why I have come? Soon I must return to fight the prince of the kingdom of Persia, and after that the spirit of the kingdom of Greece will come. Meanwhile, I will tell you what is written in the Book of Truth. (No one helps me against these spirit princes except Michael your spirit prince. I have been standing beside Michael to support and strengthen him since the first year of the reign of Darius the Mede)' (Dan. 10:1-21 NLT).

At that time Michael, the archangel, who stands guard over your nation, will arise. Then there will be a time of anguish greater than any since nations first came into existence. But at that time every one of your people whose name is written in the book will be rescued. Many of those whose bodies lie dead and buried will rise up, some to everlasting life and some to shame and everlasting disgrace. Those who are wise will shine as bright as the sky, and those who lead many to righteousness will shine like the stars forever. But you, Daniel, keep this prophecy a secret; seal up the book until the time of the end, when many will rush here and there, and knowledge will increase (Dan. 12:1-4 NLT).

GOD'S SECRET

That night the secret was revealed to Daniel in a vision. Then Daniel praised the God of heaven. He said, 'Praise the name of God forever and ever, for he has all wisdom and power. He controls the course of world events, he removes kings and sets up other kings. He gives wisdom to the wise and knowledge to the scholars. He reveals deep and mysterious things and knows what lies hidden in darkness, though he is surrounded by light. I thank and praise you, God of my ancestors, for you have given me wisdom and strength. You have told me what we asked of you and revealed to us what the king demanded' (Dan. 2:19-23) (NLT)

The king said to Daniel 'Truly, your God is the greatest of gods, the Lord over kings, a revealer of mysteries, for you have been able to reveal this secret' (Dan. 2:47 NLT).

GOD'S PROGRESSIVE REVELATION

This message was kept secret for centuries and generations past but now it has been revealed to God's people. For God wanted them to know that the riches and glory of Christ are for you Gentiles, too. And this is the secret: Christ lives in you. This gives you assurance of sharing his glory (Col. 1:26-27 NLT).

God has now revealed to us his mysterious plan regarding Christ, a plan to fulfill his own good pleasure. And this is the plan: At the right time he will bring everything together under the authority of Christ—everything in heaven and on earth" (Eph. 1:9 NLT).

And pray for me, too. Ask God to give me the right words so I can boldly explain God's mysterious plan that the Good News is for Jews and Gentiles alike. I am in chains now, still preaching this message as God's ambassador. So, pray that I will keep on speaking boldly for him, as I should (Eph. 6:19-20 NLT).

Pray for us, too, that God will give us many opportunities to speak about his mysterious plan concerning Christ. That is why I am here in chains. Pray that I will proclaim this message as clearly as I should" (Col. 4:3-4 NLT).

Without question, this is the great mystery of our faith. Christ was revealed in a human body and vindicated by the Spirit. He was seen by angels and announced to the nations. He was believed in throughout the world and taken to heaven in glory (1 Tim. 3:16 NLT).

*So, look at Apollos and me as mere servants of Christ who
have been put in charge of explaining God's mysteries (I Cor.
4:1 NLT).*

*I want you to know how much I have agonized for you and
for the church at Laodicea, and for many other believers who
have never met me personally. I want them to be encouraged
and knot together by strong ties of love. I want them to have
complete confidence that they understand God's mysterious
plan, which is Christ himself. In him lie hidden all the
treasures of wisdom and knowledge (Col. 2:1-3 NLT).*

*Now all glory to God, who is able to make you strong, just
as my Good News says. This message about Jesus Christ has
revealed his plan for you Gentiles, a plan kept secret from the
beginning of time. But now as the prophets foretold and as
the eternal God has commanded, this message is made known
to all Gentiles everywhere, so that they too might believe
and obey him. All glory to the only wise God, through Jesus
Christ, forever. Amen (Rom. 16:25-27 NLT).*

GOD'S SECRET REVEALED TODAY
WHO IS SATAN?

The word Satan is used 24 times in the Old Testament. From Job we
read,

*One day when the angels came to report to God, Satan, who
was the Designated Accuser, came along with them. God
singled out Satan and said, What have you been up to?*

*Satan answered God, 'Going here and there, checking
things out on earth.'*

*God said to Satan, 'Have you noticed my friend Job?
There's no one quite like him—honest and true to his word,
totally devoted to God and hating evil.'*

*Satan retorted, 'So do you think Job does all that out of
sheer goodness of his heart? Why, no one ever had it so good!*

You pamper him like a pet, make sure nothing bad ever happens to him or his family or his possessions, bless everything he does—he can't lose!'

'But what do you think would happen if you reached down and took away everything that is his? He'd curse you right to your face, that's what.'

God replied, 'We'll see. Go ahead—do what you want with all that is his. Just don't hurt him.' Then Satan left the presence of God. (Job 1:6-12 MSG)

We learn from Revelation that Satan is called by three names: *So that huge dragon—the ancient serpent, the one called the devil and Satan, who deceives the whole world—was thrown down to earth, and his angels along with him (Rev. 12:9 NET).*

This is the same creature we read about in Genesis.

The serpent was clever, more clever than any wild animal God had made. He spoke to the Woman: 'Do I understand that God told you not to eat from any tree in the garden?'

The Woman said to the serpent, 'Not at all. We can eat from the trees in the garden. It's only about the tree in the middle of the garden that God said, 'Don't eat from it; don't even touch it or you'll die.'

The serpent told the Woman, 'You won't die. God knows that the moment you eat from that tree, you'll see what's really going on. You'll be just like God knowing everything, ranging all the way from good to evil.'

When the Woman saw that the tree looked like good eating and realized what she could get out of it—she'd know everything—she took and ate the fruit and then gave some to her husband and he ate."

Immediately the two of them did 'see what's really going on'—saw themselves naked! They sewed fig leaves together as makeshift clothes for themselves.

When they heard the sound of God strolling in the garden in the evening breeze, the Man and his Wife hid in the trees of the garden, hid from God. God called to the Man: 'Where are you?'

He said, 'I heard you in the garden and I was afraid because I was naked. And I hid.'

God said, 'Who told you you were naked? Did you eat from that tree I told you not to eat from?'

The Man said, 'The Woman you gave me as a companion, she gave me fruit from the tree, and, yes, I ate it.'

God said to the Woman, 'What is this that you've done?'

'The serpent seduced me,' she said, and I ate.

God told the serpent: 'Because you've done this, you're cursed, cursed beyond all cattle and wild animals, cursed to slink on your belly and eat dirt all your life. I'm declaring war between you and the Woman, between your offspring and hers. He'll wound your head, and you'll wound his heel'
(Gen. 3:1-15 MSG).

From the Scriptures we learn the real conflict is because God created the freedom of choice in angels and humanity. The International Standard Bible Encyclopedia defines Satan as, "A created but superhuman, personal, evil, world-power, represented in Scriptures as the adversary both of God and men." Other comments follow. In the Old Testament Satan is not represented as a fallen and malignant spirit, but as a servant of Yahweh, performing a divine function and having his place in the heavenly train. As in Job Chapter 1 and 2 where we see him presenting himself before God accusing Job. He is superhuman, but not in any sense divine. His activities are cosmic, but not universal or transcendent. He is a created being. His power is definitely circumscribed. He is doomed to final destruction as a world-power. His entire career is that of a secondary and dependent being who is permitted a certain limited scope of power and activity (Luke 4:6).

The progressive revelation of God's character and purposes, which more and more imperatively demands that the origin of moral evil, and natural evil, must be traced to the created will in opposition to the divine will, leads to the ultimate declaration that Satan is a morally fallen being whose conquest the Divine Power in history is pledged. There is also the distinct possibility that in the transition from the Satan of the

Old Testament to that of the New Testament we have the outlines of a biography and an indication of the way by which the angels fell.

Most Bible scholars view Ezekiel 28 as the description of Satan and his fall from heaven. What amazes me is the puzzlement of God's lament as He asks why. Satan had been created good and given all the best blessings of God and Satan was "an anointed guardian cherub" and "From the day you were created you were blameless in your ways until wickedness was found in you." Satan's heart had become proud!

Another amazement to me that stands out in the Book of Ezekiel is this statement mentioned fifty-eight times: "Then they will know that I AM the Lord." The concept presented is this, obey God and you will be blessed; disobey and curse God and you will be cursed!

The War on Earth

Satan was thrown down to earth with all his angels….the accuser of our brothers and sisters…day and night…the devil is angry because he knows his time is short.

The people on earth defeat Satan by the blood of the Lamb and their testimony.

All who know God's commandments and maintain their testimony for Jesus are not afraid to die.

Chaplain (Colonel) Allen Ferry said "that of the past three thousand four hundred years, humans have been entirely at peace for only two hundred sixty years or just eight percent of this timeframe. This means mankind has been at war ninety-two percent of recorded history!" Just as tragic are the wars we fight in our personal lives. James' practical book for living includes three sources of such conflict: wrong desires, wrong friendships and wrong guidance. He also provides God's wisdom for solutions for peace" (Triad Baptist Church, July 9, 2017).

So, the War in Heaven was transferred to War on Earth. Satan was cast to earth with his rebellious following: one-third of the angels in Heaven. He was very angry when he learned his new environment and his loss of power, prestige and privileges. Satan only has limited power, the power that God gives him. Satan is now a prisoner of God's Will.

Now God's Will is to build a creature to live with Him in Heaven. A creature that would have freedom of choice, the ability to discern good from evil and had been tested and tried on earth and consistently chose to obey God because experiences on earth proved that God is who the Scriptures teach about His character.

THE LORD HAS NO EQUAL

Who else has held the oceans in his hand? Who has measured off the heavens with his fingers? Who else knows the weight of the earth or has weighed the mountains and hills on a scale? Who is able to advise the Spirit of the Lord? Who knows enough to give him advice or teach him? Has the Lord ever needed anyone's advice? Does he need instruction about what is good? Did someone teach him what is right or show him the path of justice? No, for all the nations of the world are but a drop in the bucket. They are nothing more than dust on the scales. He picks up the whole earth as though it were a grain of sand. All the wood in Lebanon's forests and all Lebanon's animals would not be enough to make a burnt offering worthy of our God. The nations of the world are worth nothing to him. In his eyes they count for less than nothing—mere emptiness and froth. To whom can you compare God? What image can you find to resemble him? Can he be compared to an idol formed in a mold, overlaid with gold, and decorated with silver chains? Or if people are too poor for that they might at least choose wood than won't decay and a skilled craftsman to carve an image that won't fall down! Haven't you heard? Don't you understand? Are you deaf to the words of God—the words he gave before the world began? Are you so ignorant? God sits above the circle of the earth. The people below seem like grasshoppers to him! He spreads out the heavens like a curtain and makes his tent from them. He judges the great people of the world and brings them all to nothing. They hardly get started, barely taking root, when he blows on them and they wither. The wind carries them off like chaff. To whom will you compare me? Who is my equal? asks the Holy One. Look up into the heavens. Who created all the stars? He brings them out like an army, one after another, calling each by its name. Because of his great power and incomparable strength, not a single one is missing. O Jacob, how can you say the Lord does not see your troubles? O Israel, how can you say God ignores your rights? Have you never heard? Have you never understood? The Lord is the everlasting God, the Creator of all the earth. He never grows weak or weary. No one can measure the depths of his understanding. He gives power to the weak and strength to the powerless. Even youths will become weak and tired, and young men will fall in exhaustion. But those who trust in the Lord will find new strength. They will soar high on wings like eagles. They will run and not grow weary. They will walk and not faint (Isa. 40:1-31 NLT).

The War in Our Minds

Pride leads to disgrace but with humility comes wisdom. — Proverbs 11:2 NLT

Fear of the Lord is the foundation of wisdom. Knowledge of the Holy One results in good judgment. — Proverbs 9:10 NLT

When they cry for help. I will not answer. Though they anxiously search for me they will not find me. For they hated knowledge and chose not to fear the Lord. They rejected my advice and paid no attention when I corrected them. Therefore, they must eat the bitter fruit of having their own way, choking on their own schemes. Proverbs 1:28-31 NLT

God created us as unique complex creatures. We are the only creatures who can speak the language of spoken words. God also gave us feelings—emotions.

With our feelings, our eyes can see, our ears can hear, our nose can smell, our mouth can taste, our nerves can touch and experience pain and pleasure, and our brain can reflect, and realize that we are a conscience living being, and can think, rationalize and make choices.

All our emotions can develop into thoughts. Thoughts develop into words. Words create actions. Actions create habits. Habits create character. Character creates destiny.

All these parts together form a great puzzle.

God's purpose for us is to have freedom of choice. Just like Adam and Eve in the Garden were presented with two alternatives: Believe God's words or believe Satan's words.

Each choice has consequences. Each thought, word, action, habit comes with buried consequences as we continue the habit of believing God or Satan. God provides the ability for us to make a choice, therefore the consequences are our very own choice and not God's choice. We cannot blame God for our own bad choices.

> *People may be right in their own eyes, but the Lord examines their heart (Prov. 21:2 NLT).*
>
> *The Lord directs our steps, so why try to understand everything along the way (Prov. 19:21 NLT).*
>
> *You can make many plans, but the Lord's purpose will prevail. (Prov. 19:2 NLT)*

Yes, the stair-steps of our own choices: thoughts, words, actions, habits, lead to our own buried consequences; our destiny.

Do you rule your feelings, or let your feelings rule you?

In my early twenties, when I was married with three small children, my husband came home for lunch. While he was home for lunch one day, we got into a heated argument. I cannot remember what the argument was about except it was emotionally charged. I shouted. He refused to answer. He quickly headed for his sports car and sped away.

At that time, we lived on Edwards Air Force Base in the middle of the Mojave Desert. He worked in a heavily guarded area several miles away from our home. In a fit of rage, I quickly peeked into the bedrooms and saw that our three babies were all asleep. I ran out the door and headed for our 1956 Ford Station Wagon. I was determined to catch him before he arrived behind the heavily guarded gate where he worked.

As I heavily stepped on the gas pedal, my thoughts were consumed with my urgency to force him to listen to my complaints. After a few moments, I felt like I was flying! I looked down at the speedometer and saw that I was traveling over one hundred miles per hour.

A strong voice urged me to think again. The voice said, "You fool! What are you thinking?" Then something caused me to ease up on the gas pedal. In a moment, I started shaking. A cold sweat covered my forehead. I stopped the car. I thanked God for saving me from a disastrous situation. I turned around in shame and headed home to see if my babies were safe.

Even today, sixty-two years later, I remember this. I thank God for saving me from myself. I thank God for his mercy and faithful love to me when I did not deserve it. From that time on, when I feel angry thoughts erupting, I force myself to stop. Wait. Catch my breath. Tell myself to not act. Keep calm. Through the years, in a progressive way, God has taught me how to better handle my weakness in this area. Do I still get tripped up sometime? Yes, however, when I remember to use this pattern, I overcome my anger and thank God for His mercy.

A news article caught my attention today. An established professional young man in his forties went from his hometown in the Midwest to New York. On a certain Sunday, he chose to go to a bar. He chose to drink alcohol. He chose to get into a heated argument with a stranger outside the bar. He chose to punch the stranger in the head. The stranger fell backwards, hit his head on a rock and died. Now this accomplished professional is charged with murder in New York. Yes, the stair-steps of our own choices lead to our destiny.

Years ago at a certain church, I attended a Sunday night small group meeting. We had a Bible Study, great discussions and later we enjoyed a meal with many kinds of desserts. One evening the greatest dessert choice was chocolate-covered-strawberries. Yes, they were delicious. One woman in the group weighed about three hundred fifty pounds. At the end of the class, she darted to the bowl of leftover chocolate-covered strawberries and asked to take some home. Not many days later, I was stunned to learn that this woman had been sitting at her computer viewing Facebook, with her bowl of chocolate-covered strawberries by her side, when she died. She was about the age of my children! I was grieved because we had been such good friends. Now, many years later, I still remember and grieve her passing. Yes, the stair-steps of our own choices lead to our destiny.

Are you scared to face your destiny because you have made a series of bad choices?

Jesus Christ has some Good News for you! However, you can only take advantage of this Good News by admitting with a humble heart that you need help. God's mercy only extends to people with a humble heart who call out to Him for his mercy.

> *I thank Christ Jesus our Lord, who has given me strength to do his work. He considered me trustworthy and appointed me to serve him even though I used to blaspheme the name of Christ. In my insolence, I persecuted his people. But God had mercy on me because I did it in ignorance and unbelief.*

Oh, how generous and gracious our Lord was! He filled me with the faith and love that came from Christ Jesus. This is a trustworthy saying, and everyone should accept it: "Christ Jesus came into the world to save sinners"—and I am the worst of them all. But God had mercy on me so that Christ Jesus could use me as a prime example of his great patience with even the worse sinners. Then others will realize that they too, can believe in him and receive eternal life. All honor and glory to God forever and ever! He is the eternal king, the unseen one who never dies, he alone is God. Amen (1 Tim. 1:12-17 NLT).

REFLECTIONS

---

1. Read Psalm 139:19-22 and Deuteronomy 29:29.

2. Pray that God would help you to understand His Words.

3. Do you spend time reflecting about God and how the creation happened? Do you wonder about secrets and mysteries in the Bible?

4. Read Revelation 12:7-12 and Revelation 12:17. Ask God to help you to understand.

5. Reflect on the character studies of Michael, Satan and Christ.

6. Reflect on the progressive revelation of God as revealed in these Scriptures.

7. Reflect on the number of years wars have been on earth.

8. Read and reflect on the Satan's Work on Earth Chart. When has Satan attacked you? Write the experience in your journal. How did you respond? Would you respond the same way today? Why or why not?

9. Reflect on Jesus Christ's work on earth.

10. Reflect on the war in your mind. Read 1 Timothy 1:12-17.

11. What are your thoughts?

12. Reflect on the Stair-steps to Destiny Chart in Appendix 1 - Charts

13. Review the Battles of Life Chart in Appendix 1 - Charts

14. Reflect now on a bad choice you made. Did God save you from yourself at that time? Did you react by blaming someone else? Did you face the fact that you made a bad mistake sinning against God? Did you go to God quickly to ask Him to forgive you, correct you and head you in a different direction?

CHAPTER 9

My Breath-Taking Experience
November 7, 2011

Search me, O God, and know my heart; test me and know
my anxious thoughts. Point out anything in me that offends
you, and lead me along the path of everlasting life
—Psalm 139: 23-24

On Sunday morning November 7, 2011, I watched Dr. David Jeremiah's television program called Turning Point. He had just published a book called, *I Never Thought That I'd See the Day!*

That morning, he was preaching from Chapter 8, <u>When a Muslim State Could Intimidate the World</u>. As I watched the program, some of his key concepts caused me to have a flashback to an event that took place September 30, 2001. The following is the backstory.

EARLY 1970'S

Harold was called to serve as the preacher of a struggling church in Kentucky. We moved there from New Jersey just a few days after our oldest daughter, Deborah was married. The move from New Jersey was quite an experience. Harold rented a twenty-two- foot Ryder moving van and towed our old truck that we affectionately called Caledonia. She was loaded to top capacity. We drove in a caravan of four cars and two trucks. Our two married daughters and their husbands, a kitten, Cathy, John,

Harold's Mother, Harold and me and our two dogs - a Saint Bernard and a Keeshond.

We had a terrific trip with no problems. However, when we pulled into the church parking lot in Kentucky, Caledonia had a flat tire. When Harold inspected the trailer hitch on the Ryder Truck, he found that it was broken and rusty. Inspecting farther, he was stunned. The trailer hitch had never been screwed down properly. In other words, the truck could have come unhitched any time as we breezed up and down the mountains for six hundred miles. Yes, God really cared for us on that journey!

After we arrived and started working with that little church group, we experienced many challenges in our family life and church life. In our family life, it took time to adjust to the new culture. Our three married daughters living in California, Idaho and New Jersey moved to Kentucky. Our second year, we experienced the birth of three grandchildren. Cathy moved from high school to the University of Kentucky and John was in high school. Harold had a heart attack. We celebrated our 25th Wedding Anniversary. I worked in a civil engineering firm thirty miles away and later in an accounting firm near our home.

The church work was very demanding but rewarding. The first year over forty-one people accepted Jesus Christ as their Lord and Savior. The Sunday morning attendance jumped to over three hundred. Harold had a daily devotional radio program. The classroom facilities were expanded. The leaders agreed to purchase fifty-two acres on beautiful rolling green hills to build a parsonage that would later become a retirement center, and then later a new sanctuary. Soon they purchased one hundred fifty acres nearby for a church campsite.

Harold's work was grueling as he taught several weekly Bible classes, preached two weekly sermons, and conducted the daily radio program. He also supervised the construction. He enjoyed so much working alongside the construction workers.

As the years rolled by, the church continued to expand. We began to be very frustrated with so many conflicting, important activities to juggle, feelings of not being able to complete anything well, not being able to spend quality time with family and our relationship as husband and wife. We saw no relief in sight. We prayed.

During these circumstances, we were saddened to learn that two of our married daughters would be moving back to California. We had lived there years before when they were growing up for twelve years. We decided that we needed a break, craved time alone, continued our prayers, and then elected to head to Florida and find a different work, had no definite plans but just decided to go and see what happened. We prayed continually, traveled along and God showed us his plan. We would move to North Carolina and not continue to Florida.

FAST FORWARD TO SEPTEMBER 30, 2001

July of 2001, the Kentucky church contacted Harold and asked him to conduct a week-long gospel meeting for them. We had not kept up with the progress of this church. We were very busy at that time fully engaged in a large church building project in Dawsonville, Georgia. However, Harold told them he would do the meeting. After many prayers, Harold decided that the theme of the week would be *God's Unfailing Love*.

The mood of the entire United States was raw September 11 due to the bombing of the Twin Towers in New York City. The future seemed unthinkable and dark. Everyone was either consciously or unconsciously trying to make sense of this horrible event. When we arrived in Kentucky it was only nineteen days after this great tragedy. So, everyone listening to Harold's sermons and Bible Class messages were at the same time trying to make sense of this recent tragic event.

This process is called Cognitive Dissonance. This is the anxiety that results from simultaneously holding contradictory thoughts or incompatible attitudes and beliefs. Harold chose to try to find thoughts from the Bible and to see this situation from God's perspective. Some of his key concepts were these.

The Muslims are the descendants of Esau. He gave examples of how God had sometimes used the Muslims to punish Israel when the people disobeyed God.

Harold then warned the people, "Search your hearts. Look inside to see if your thoughts are pleasing to God." He explained that Muslims were Persians. He asked the audience to read the beautiful book of Esther in the Old Testament. He explained that this tells how God protected his people during trying times. Next, he shared how we had taught Muslims in Ghana about Jesus and how many were open to this great message of love.

About this time, in the middle of Harold's sermon, my thoughts drifted off to one of our memorable experiences in Ghana working with people who were Muslims. This is an experience I copied from my book, *Trailblazing with God, Learning to Walk on the Water.* These were two letters that I wrote to my parents.

OCTOBER 13, 1964 — GHANA, WEST AFRICA

We went to Obuasi last Sunday. Obuasi is a gold mining town with a population of about twenty-six- thousand and boasts of having the largest gold mine in the world. The mine employs six thousand people. This is the original mine and they go down seven hundred feet to get gold. It is a beautiful town and very clean. Most of the population is Muslim.

The congregation in Obuasi was started three or four years ago and fell away. Recently one of the new preaching students started contacting some of the brethren there. On Sunday, we had a large attendance with five very influential men attending. One of the men, Brother Appiah, manages a fishing corporation. He recently built a new store building with living quarters attached. He announced that he had never been successful until he became a Christian. Now that God has blessed him so abundantly, he wants to give the church the store building for worship services and the living quarters for a preacher's home. The student preacher in Obuasi is a former Muslim. We are so pleased about the work. Pray for them.

SUNDAY APRIL 11, 1965

We went to church this morning at Obuasi. It was the last time we could go there. Everyone told us good-bye. They were all so sweet and it was difficult to think we can't go back to see them. Sister Appiah gave Cathy her gold necklace and they gave us pineapples, bananas and oranges. We went to Brother Appiah's for refreshments. Good-byes are always difficult.

With these fond memories in my heart, suddenly, the sound of people singing the closing hymn brought me back to reality—to this Kentucky church now. I stood up, walked to the church entrance and stood by my husband as we greeted people leaving the service. Later we were silently led to the fellowship building by two of the leaders we did not know.

Afterward in the fellowship building the crowd acted restless, apprehensive and fearful as they silently walked through the buffet line selecting their food. We watched as they pooled together in small intimate groups at one of the many tables. We selected our food and found two empty chairs at a table with a young couple with two small children. The children were restless, and the couple tried to get them to eat. When they made excuses for their children's behavior, Harold responded by telling the children funny stories. We all laughed.

Soon one of the leaders approached us and asked Harold to come with him to a meeting with the elders. I watched in silence as they all walked outside. After a long wait, Harold returned to the table and sat down beside me. I could feel his anxiety, see his red face and his eyes darted around the room. He leaned over and whispered, "We need to leave."

When we returned to our room, he explained to me that the meeting was filled with strong disagreements. They were quite uncertain how to move forward. Some leaders wanted him to preach the Sunday evening sermon and some did not. They finally decided to let him preach. Harold then told me he needed time to review the evening message, so I went to the bedroom to read.

At the appointed time, we went to the church sanctuary for the evening service. I chose to sit near the back, observe and pray silently. When Harold began his sermon, I realized that he had gone back to his favorite sermon series on the Parables of Jesus. He picked the parable of the unforgiving debtor (Matt. 18: 21-35).

Bright and early the next morning, we heard a loud knock on the front door where we were staying. When Harold opened the door, the elders and the treasurer came in. Harold encouraged them to sit in the living room where they could talk. I remained in the bedroom. I sat on the side of the bed too stunned to move. I quietly listened to their loud conversation. I heard them strongly threaten Harold to leave immediately! Never come back! Never contact them again!

I could hear Harold's voice softly responding in his usual gentle manner to the gruff loud voices. They were angry. Harold was gentle.

I froze. I could not believe my ears. Next, I heard the door slam. They were gone. When Harold walked into the bedroom, he put the thousand dollars check in my lap. He gazed at my troubled face and asked, "Why?" I looked away in silence.

We grieved going home. I grieved throughout the many years that followed, not knowing why. I was puzzled even a few weeks before Harold's death. A few months after Harold's passing, I decided to contact the elders and ask them why. Harold would not let me do it before. I wrote. No answer. It turned out that most of the people involved in the incident had died. My question remained unanswered.

SUNDAY MORNING NOVEMBER 7, 2011

Believing I had processed this devastating hurt, I went to the Bible Curriculum Task Force/Bible Teacher meeting. As a member of this team, I had been asked to help prepare the Bible curriculum for the entire church for the next year. I was very excited about this meeting because I was in the beginning stages of writing this book. They had accepted an outline I had prepared. Andrew Baker, another member of this team, did a superb job of taking my outline, making sense of it, and writing information the Bible Teachers could use for every week of the first quarter of 2012. He handed out the detailed packet for us to review.

After class, I asked for a meeting with David Jernigan, one of the leaders. We met alone in the conference room in the front of the church. With Andrew Baker's packet in hand, I needed to ask David some questions.

Once seated, my mind instantly flashed to David Jeremiah's television message I had heard earlier that morning, when something strange happened. Suddenly without warning, I began sobbing. The deep crying continued for quite a while. Finally, my sobbing was controlled, and I found myself pouring out my pain of the Kentucky incident. I was grateful to David Jernigan for the gift of his listening ear, calmness, gentleness, concern and caring. He was a blessing to me that day. David gave me a great place to think out loud. His listening gave me the opportunity to reveal my deep hurts to someone who really cared. Acknowledging the pain, deeply feeling it, releasing the pain with an outpouring of tears had lifted a heavy burden that had been weighing me down for a long time.

The relief I felt was amazing; a catharsis that healed me. This Bible verse best explains my feelings:

> *So, humble yourselves under the mighty power of God, and at the right time he will lift you up in honor. Give all your worries and cares to God, for he cares about you. Stay alert! Watch out for your great enemy, the devil. He prowls around like a roaring lion, looking for someone to devour. Stand firm against him and be strong in your faith. Remember that your Christian brothers and sisters all over world are going through the same kind of suffering you are. In his kindness God called you to share in his eternal glory by means of Christ Jesus. So, after you have suffered a little while, he will restore support, and strengthen you and he will place you on a firm foundation. All power to him forever! Amen (1 Peter 5:6-11).(NLT)*

Once home, I settled into my favorite chair to reflect. The scene in that conference room was still fresh. I was struck with the perfection of God's timing—providing the perfect place and loving, listening ears. I now felt whole. The fragment I'd left behind in that small town was finally reclaimed.

The next day I got a phone call from an assistant at Chancellor Michael Milton's office at the Reformed Theological Seminary asking me how I liked the book that he had sent. Evidently the book was lost in the mail. He said the name of the book is called, *Hit by Friendly Fire* by Dr. Michael A. Milton. He immediately sent another book. When the book arrived, I found the message to be powerful—showing me how to overcome adversity. The following thoughts are gems I gained after reading Dr. Milton's book.

TAKE UP MY CROSS

After much reflection and many prayers, I wondered: What is my cross? I began to realize God had been progressively teaching me. Next, this Bible verse popped into my mind: *If you think you are standing strong, be careful not to fall (I Cor. 10:12).*

When I think of the word falling, it reminds me of an incident I had several years ago. This incident happened at church. Here is the story I told in my book, *God's House! Beautiful! Let's Go!*

I was walking toward the entrance of church on a Sunday morning near the end of March, speaking to a visitor, when I stepped up onto the curb, I lost my balance, and fell. I was stunned. I had fallen on my right side and could not move!

Immediately I was surrounded by a host of people trying to figure out how to help me. The look of concern on their faces terrified me. What had happened? What was I going to do now?

Before I could contemplate the answers, someone rolled over a wheelchair to transport me to the church office. Soon I was surrounded by three compassionate nurses. They put my arm in a temporary sling and put ice on my elbow. They took my blood pressure and examined me for other wounds. They washed my bloody face and examined my jaw and the side of my head that had hit the concrete. Someone found my daughter Diana, who was already seated in the sanctuary, and brought her to the office. She whisked me away to the emergency room. There it was determined I had broken my right elbow and big toe. They treated the bloody scrapes and lacerations on my face and encouraged me to see my family physician the next day.

Immediately—from one footstep to the next—my world had changed! Harold had always said when you pray for specific needs, fasten your seat belt, because God will answer your request—although not necessarily in the way you expect, so you will know the answer came from God.

Very soon I discovered my entire mindset had changed. I was dependent on others to help me. I discovered that accepting help was more painful than my injuries. Before falling I had no idea my stubborn pride was such a problem!

God taught me many valuable lessons as friends took me to church, the doctor, the grocery store, the post office, the bank, cleaned my house and prepared my meals. I worked one day a week at an accounting office, and the owners, Jim and Randy picked me up for work and took me home. Our son, John, told me I should not rob these people of the joy God gives them from serving.

I wondered if God felt the same way about our accepting the grace that he has provided for us through his Son Jesus Christ. Does our stubborn pride say, "I'll do it myself!" Does this attitude get in the way of our believing and accepting God's grace? I didn't know this pride was in me before my fall.

I learned a valuable lesson about the Kingdom of God. We are not lone rangers on this journey through life. God provided the church which is made up of believers in Jesus Christ. These followers should cling together in the bonds of unity and peace with a spirit of helping others. We're all traveling the same journey. The church is the Bride of Christ and moves in harmony with God the Father, God the Son and God the Holy Spirit. Christ is praying that we all follow his example.

The above concept is worth thinking about. Do we accept the precious gift of salvation that Jesus Christ offers us? We were his enemies when he died on the cross to forgive our sins and make us acceptable so we could live with God in Heaven. Believing and sharing is our part of this great responsibility and mystery."

I sat reflecting and then decided to open my Bible. God spoke to me again:

> *The human heart is the most deceitful of all things, and desperately wicked. Who really knows how bad it is? But I, the Lord, search all hearts and examine secret motives. I give all people their due rewards according to what their actions deserve (Jer. 17:9-10).*

> *Then Jesus said, "Come to me, all of you who are weary and carry heavy burdens, and I will give you rest. Take my yoke upon you. Let me teach you, because I am humble [emphasis mine] and gentle at heart, and you will find rest for your souls. For my yoke is easy to bear and the burden I give you is light (Matt. 11:28-30).*

The word humble pierced my soul, and I wondered what Christ was thinking before his cross. I turned to John and read:

> *After saying all these things, Jesus looked up to heaven and said, "Father, the hour has come. Glorify your Son so, he*

*can give glory back to you. For you have given him authority
over everyone. He gives eternal life to each one you have given
him. And this is the way to have eternal life to know you, the
only true God, and Jesus Christ, the one you sent to earth.
I brought glory to you here on earth by completing the work
you gave me to do. Now, Father bring me into the glory we
shared before the world began (John 17:1-4) (NLT)*

WHO IS THIS JESUS CHRIST?

*Christ is the visible image of the invisible God. He existed
before anything was created and is supreme over all creation.
For through him God created everything in the heavenly
realms and on earth. He made the things we can see and
the things we can't see—such as thrones, kingdoms, rulers
and authorities in the unseen world. Everything was created
through him and for him. He existed before anything else,
and he holds all creation together. Christ is also the head of
the church which is his body. He is the beginning Supreme
over all who rise from the dead. So, he is first in everything.
For God in all his fullness was pleased to live in Christ, and
through him God reconciled everything to himself. He made
peace with everything in heaven and on earth by means of
Christ's blood on the cross (Col. 1:15-16) (NLT)*

HOW CAN I KNOW CHRIST?

After reading the above Scripture, and reflecting more deeply, I
remembered how much the Apostle Paul wrote about this. I turned to his
words to the Galatians:

*My old self has been crucified with Christ. It is no longer I
who live, but Christ lives in me. So, I live in this earthly body
by trusting in the Son of God, who loved me and gave himself
for me. I do not treat the grace of God as meaningless. For*

if keeping the law could make us right with God, then there was no need for Christ to die (Gal. 2:20-21) (NLT).

From now on, don't let anyone trouble me with these things. For I bear in my body the scars that show I belong to Christ (Gal. 6:17).

I instantly realized in finally dealing with the hurtful incident in Kentucky an avalanche of emotions crashed down—rejection, loss and painful acts I'd carried for all these subsequent years. Now I felt humbled. God had healed me. He had used circumstances, people, my ability to remember and contemplate. He had respected my ability to choose to go to His Word, pray and listen. When I opened my Bible, my scars began to look like stars, and I saw Jesus telling me I belonged to him. A true peace settled over my soul.

Take Off My Crown

The word "take" implies a choice. God gave each of us the power of freedom of choice. This power comes with responsibility. Everything we say, do or think has a rippling effect in our life—producing consequences we don't have the power to control. We are all just one step away from disaster or victory.

Facebook posted a picture and underneath the picture was a heartbreaking story showing the consequence of a choice. The picture featured a beautiful, young, intelligent woman driving to work on a busy highway. She chose to take a selfie while she was driving. The second that her selfie was posted on Facebook, she completely lost control of her car and swerved into the oncoming lane of another vehicle. The impact of this accident killed the young woman instantly.

What was she thinking? She was certainly not thinking in the now. She was a lazy unthinking slave driven by her selfish pride of fame. Where did these feelings lead? Do our thinking patterns lead to mood swings, unhealthy desires for a rush of adrenaline, or a desire for more intense feelings?

Jane Ann Derr

How do we try to resolve this?

Solomon, King David's son who ruled in Jerusalem, wrote much about this sobering question in the book of Ecclesiastes. Solomon set out to learn everything he could about wisdom, but in the end, he decided this was like chasing the wind—greater wisdom gives greater grief and sorrow. Wisdom does not bring peace.

Next Solomon explored pleasure. God had given him more than any other king. Still he discovered that pleasure does not bring peace.

He weighed the contrast of the wise and the fool or in other words, the good and the evil. He was greatly puzzled because both ended up in the grave. He wondered if it was profitable to be wise or good. This was a great puzzlement to Solomon like chasing the wind.

Then he thought about his efforts gained by skill and hard work. He questioned the value of this effort because someday it could all be taken away. His other questions were the injustices in life because people die like animals. It's like chasing the wind.

He pondered the futility of political power. As a king, endless crowds stood around him, but then another generation rejected him. This is also like chasing the wind. He described the futility of wealth and power and concluded with:

And it is a good thing to receive wealth from God and the good health to enjoy it. To enjoy your work and accept your lot in life—this is indeed a gift from God. God keeps such people so busy enjoying life that they take no time to brood over the past.

> *Enjoy what you have rather than desiring what you don't have. Just dreaming about nice things is meaningless—like chasing the wind (Eccl. 5:19-20; 6:9).*

Solomon concludes with:

A wise person thinks a lot about death,
While a fool thinks only about having a good time.
Not a single person on earth is always good and never sins.
In Ecclesiastes chapter 12, Solomon mentions the word "remember"

seven times. In the Hebrew language, the number seven means complete. Great emphasis is being placed on this concept. All the concepts in the book of Ecclesiastes hang on this word. Then Solomon's conclusion is:

That's the whole story. Here now is my conclusion: Fear God and obey his commands, for this is everyone's duty. God will judge us for everything we do, including every secret thing, whether good or bad (Eccl. 12:13-14).(NLT)

Look! I am creating new heavens and a new earth, and no one will even think about the old ones anymore (Isa. 65:17) (NLT)

Go To My Gethsemane

The humble heart of Jesus led him to his daily practice of going to his Father in prayer. He spoke words to his Heavenly Father. These words became his daily habit. This habit became a set activity that preceded the destiny which was unfolding just before he went to the cross. This is his prayer:

Then Jesus went with them to the olive garden called Gethsemane, and he said, "Sit here while I go over there to pray." He took Peter and Zebedee's two sons, James and John, and he became anguished and distressed. He told them, "My soul is crushed with grief to the point of death. Stay here and keep watch with me." He went on a little farther and bowed with his face to the ground, praying, "My Father! If it is possible, let this cup of suffering be taken away from me. Yet, I want your will to be done, not mine." Then he returned to the disciples and found them asleep. He said to Peter, "Couldn't you watch with me even one hour? Keep watch and pray, so that you will not give in to temptation. For the spirit is willing, but the body is weak!" (Matt. 26:36-40).

After saying all these things, Jesus looked up to heaven and said, "Father, the hour has come. Glorify your Son so he can give glory back to you. For you have given him authority over everyone. He gives eternal life to each one you have given to him. And this is the way to have eternal life, to know you, the only true God, and Jesus Christ, the one you sent to earth. I brought glory to you here on earth by completing the work you gave me to do. Now, Father, bring me into the glory we shared before the world began" (John 17:1-4) (NLT).

When I reflect on my personal Gethsemane, I immediately remember this scene. It was 1939. I was in bed. The room was dark except for the light bulb hanging from a wire in the ceiling. Mother had taken a newspaper and made a lampshade over the light bulb. This light was bright enough for me to read. I would hide books under my pillow so I could read at night when everything was quiet. My favorite book was my Bible. I had deep feelings about the Bible. It was precious to me. The words calmed my deepest fears. Why was I terrified? Why did I hide my Bible?

I was born January 1933 and the same month Adolph Hitler was appointed Chancellor of Germany. We lived in Terre Haute, Indiana at 811 South Third Street. Our next-door neighbors were Charley and Isdore Gurman. Their father Israel had started Gurman Container and Supply Corporation and his sons worked with him in the family business.

The Gurman's had a favorite apple tree in their backyard. My brother, Jack and I enjoyed knocking the apples to the ground and then we made a game of throwing the apples, trying to hit each other. Mrs. Gurman solved the problem. She told us that we should not destroy her apples. She said that she would give us desserts she had made from the apples, called Bratapfel, if we would not bother her apple tree. We immediately stopped destroying her apples and looked forward to our weekly dessert.

This was during the Great Depression. We were poor so we were overjoyed with our weekly dessert. In addition, the oldest son, Charley would take us to the ice cream parlor across the street. He would treat us to any flavor of ice cream that we wanted!

Very soon, the younger son, Isidore went into the Army. I remember hearing the adults discuss passionately their fears about what was going on in Germany. Our family listened daily to the news on the radio. At the age of seven, I remember hearing discussions that Germany had invaded

Poland and Adolph Hitler had deported German Jews to Poland. The adult men were terrified about what all of this meant.

When I was eight, I heard discussions about why the Germans had set up concentration camps in Auschwitz. Daddy and Charley Gurman had many discussions about the fate of the German Jews. Charley was concerned about the fate of his family in Germany. Daddy and Charley were both terrified about the future of the Jews and about our future. They felt burdened by the Great Depression and now these events going on in Europe added to their concerns.

I was too terrified to talk to anyone about this except Mother. She would always look away from me and then change the subject. She told us to go to the Bible every day and God would help us. So, we read the Bible and prayed. Mother was an avid Bible reader and her favorite scripture was:

Every word of God proves true. He is a shield to all who come to him for protection. Do not add to his words or he may rebuke you and expose you as a liar (Prov. 30:5-6) (NLT)

Mother said this verse helped her when she was afraid. She had gone to this verse many times when her daddy came home drunk and beat her mother. She and her two sisters would escape to the cornfield and hide. Her story made me shutter. I decided I should hide my Bible under my pillow so no one would steal it. I read it every night and prayed to God to keep me safe. The words made me feel calm and soon I would go to sleep.

When I deeply contemplate some of my prayers and compare them to Jesus prayers, they are all pale compared to His. As I compare, two great concepts weigh heavy on my soul: Christ's concept of humility and his concept of forgiveness.

HUMILITY

Christ's concept of a humble heart runs like a scarlet thread all the way through the entire Bible. Some of these threads are in the books of Isaiah, Proverbs, and James.

The high and lofty one who lives in eternity, the Holy One, says this: "I live in the high and holy place with those whose spirits are contrite and humble. I restore the crushed spirit of the humble and revive the courage of those with repentant hearts (Isa. 57:15).

My hands have made both heaven and earth; they and everything in them are mine. I, the Lord, have spoken! "I will bless those who have humble and contrite hearts, who tremble at my word (Isa. 66:2) (NLT)

Pride leads to disgrace, but with humility comes wisdom (Prov. 11:2).

True humility and fear of the Lord lead to riches, honor, and long life (Prov. 22:3).

Pride ends in humiliation, while humility brings honor (Prov. 29:23).

People who conceal their sins will not prosper, but if they confess and turn from them, they will receive mercy (Prov. 28:13).

God opposes the proud but favors the humble. So, humble yourselves before God. Resist the devil, and he will flee from you. Come close to God and God will come close to you (James 4:5-7).

FORGIVENESS

Knowing Christ means having the God-given ability to embrace the concept of forgiveness. One of the most difficult statements we make is to admit we made a mistake. So, we can readily see that forgiveness is closely linked to a humble spirit.

It can be difficult to extend forgiveness in many very painful situations. However, with God's power through His Word and the Holy Spirit living within us, forgiveness is possible! *That's the resurrection power!*

I don't know about you, but it is so easy for me to ignore the obvious – just block it out and pretend it is not there – things hidden in plain sight.

I believe God is telling me to focus now on what it means to have a forgiving spirit. Forgiveness is the golden key that opens heaven's pearly gates. *Accepting God's forgiveness is contingent on our forgiving the people in our daily life.* Now let's go to the Bible and see what we can find:

> *Jesus said, "Father, forgive them for they don't know what they are doing." And the soldiers gambled for his clothes by throwing dice (Luke 23:34).*

> *Oh, what joy for those whose disobedience is forgiven, whose sins are put out of sight. Yes, what joy for those who record the Lord has cleared of sin (Rom. 4:7-8) (Ps. 32)*

> *Oh, what joy for those whose disobedience is forgiven, whose sin is put out of sight! Yes, what joy for those whose record the Lord has cleared of guilt, whose lives are lived in complete honesty! When I refused to confess my sin, my body wasted away, and I groaned all day long. Day and night your hand of discipline was heavy on me. My strength evaporated like water in the summer heat. (Ps. 32:1-4)*

> *But when you are praying, first forgive anyone you are holding a grudge against, so that your Father in heaven will forgive your sins, too (Mark 11:25).*

> *Get rid of all bitterness, rage, anger, harsh words, and slander, as well as all types of evil behavior. Instead, be kind to each other, tenderhearted, forgiving one another, just as God through Christ has forgiven you (Eph. 4:32).*

> *Make allowance for each other's faults and forgive anyone who offends you. Remember, the Lord forgave you, so you must forgive others (Col. 3:13).*

Amid all my circumstances, past, present and future, God was gently teaching me a great truth. He handpicked every moment so I would forever understand His will and heal from the burden of pride and un-forgiveness.

EMBRACED BY GOD'S AMAZING GRACE

WHAT GOD HAS DONE
Always remember the big picture.

TO ME
Transformed my life.

FOR ME
Provided all the money, friends, and circumstances to equip me.

WITH ME
Used me to be an instrument to reach others.

Do you think you are wasting time—killing time—when you stop to read the Bible and pray? No! Not praying leads to endless circles and exhausting you, and then you end up drained of emotional energy. By not praying, you will be missing out on the wonderful peace, energy, excitement, fresh discoveries and great new possibilities that God has planned for your life.

God gifted us all with the ability of freedom of choice. We can surrender our will to God's Will or not—choosing instead to follow our own whims. Are there changes that you want to make but haven't? Seriously consider this question, and how it relates to your life right now. The answer to this question may change your life in ways unimaginable.

REFLECTIONS

---

1. Read Psalm 139:23-24

2. Pray that God would give you understanding.

3. Read Jeremiah 17:9-10. Pray and think about the deceitfulness of the human heart. Ask God to reveal to you the part of you that is deceitful where Satan has blinded in you.

4. Take up your cross.

5. Take off your crown

6. Go to your Gethsemane

7. Study Humility

8. Study Forgiveness

PART FIVE
How to Begin Your Journey with Joy

PRAY, READ, REFLECT AND
ENTER YOUR THOUGHTS HERE

PSALM 139
(NLT)

O, Lord, you have examined my heart and know everything about me. (1)

You know when I sit down or stand up. You know my thoughts even when I'm far away. (2)

You see me when I travel and when I rest at home. You know everything I do. (3)

You know what I am going to say even before I say it. Lord. (4)

You go before me and follow me. You place your hands of blessings on my head. (5)

Such knowledge is too wonderful for me, too great for me to understand. (6)

I can never escape from your Spirit! I can never get away from your presence! (7)

If I go up to heaven, you are there; if I go down to the grave, you are there. (8)

If I ride the wings of the morning, if I dwell by the farthest oceans, even there your hand will guide me, and your strength will support me. (9-10)

I could ask the darkness to hide me and the light around me to become night but even in darkness I cannot hide from you. To you the night shines as bright as day. Darkness and light are the same to you. (11-12)

You made all the delicate, inner parts of my body and knit me together in my mother's womb. Thank you for making me so wonderfully complex! Your workmanship is marvelous—how well I know it. (13-14)

You watched me as I was being formed in utter seclusion, as I was woven together in the dark of the womb. You saw me before I was born. Every day of my life was recorded in your book. Every moment was laid out before a single day had passed. (15-16)

How precious are your thoughts about me, O God, they cannot be numbered! I can't even count them; they outnumber the grains of sand! And when I wake up, you are still with me! (17-18)

O God, if only you would destroy the wicked! Get out of my life, you murderers! They blaspheme you, your enemies misuse your name. O Lord, shouldn't I hate those who hate you?

Shouldn't I despise those who oppose you? Yes, I hate them with total hatred for your enemies are my enemies. (19-22)

Search me, O God, and know my heart; test me and know my anxious thoughts. Point out anything in me that offends you and lead me along the path of everlasting life. (23-24)

Notes

PREFACE

1. Derr, Jane Ann *Trailblazing with God: learning to Walk on the Water,* Xulon Press, Longwood, Florida 2008
2. Derr, Jane Ann *God's House! Beautiful! Let's Go!* Xulon Press, Longwood, Florida, 2011
3. Rosscup. Jim, *An Exposition of Prayer,* Old Testament, Volume 2, Page 8
4. Supporting Scriptures: Job 19:23-24; Heb. 13:8; Ps 139; Prov. 28:7; Ps. 32

INTRODUCTION

1. Prov. 30:5-6 NLT
2. Rom. 8:28 NAS
3. Amos 8:11 NLT
4. Psalm 139:1-24 AMP

PART ONE
GOD'S OMNISCIENCE
Supporting Scriptures
I Kings 8:39; Ps. 139:1-4; 15-16; Isa. 46:9-10; Matt. 9:4; 10:29-30; 12:25; Mark 2:6-8; John 1:47-48; Acts 1:24; I John 3:20

FROM CHAOS TO CALM

1. Ps. 139:1 NLT
2. Ps. 119:11 NLT
3. Rom. 8:28 NLT

4. Critchlow, Loran Richard, Autobiography requested by his daughter Jane Ann Derr and letters to Jane Ann from March 9, 1981 to February 20, 1993. He died March 19, 1993.
5. Ps. 11:3-4 NLT
6. Col. 1:15-17 NLT
7. Rom. 5:6 NLT
8. Rom. 5:11 NLT

THE INVISIBLE HAND OF GOD

1. Ps. 139:2 NLT
2. Ps. 8:3-5 NLT
3. Ex. 4:10-16 NLT
4. McDermott, Gerald R. *Famous Stutterers,* 2016 Cascade Books, an Imprint of Wipt and Stock Publishers, 199 W. 8th Ave. Suite 3, Eugene, Or.
5. Derr, Jane Ann, *God's House! Beautiful! Let's Go*! Xulon Press, 2011, Pages 164-168
6. John 1:1-5 ESV
7. John 1:14 ESV
8. Vincent, Marvin R. *Word Studies in the New Testament*, Volume II, The Writings of John, Pages 23-35
9. Supporting Scriptures: Ps. 103:1-2; 11-19 NLT
10. Supporting Scripture: Ps 32

SURPRISED BY A SUDDEN STORM

1. Supporting Scripture: Ps. 139:3 NLT
2. Supporting Scripture: Ps. 40:16 NLT
3. Phillips, J. B. *The New Testament in Modern English.* J.B. 1958, The Macmillan Company 1952, 1957; Matt. 6:19-34; 1 Pet. 5:5-6; I Pet. 5:7
4. Supporting Scriptures: Heb. 13:2; Heb. 1:14; Matt. 6:14-15.

THE DAWN OF A NEW DAY

1. Ps. 139: 4-6 NLT
2. Ps. 119:117 NLT
3. Phil. 4:8 NLT
4. 1 Sam. 16:23 NLT
5. 1 Cor.14:15 NLT
6. 1 Peter 5:7 NLT
7. Jer. 1:4- 5 NLT

8. Ps. 56:1-13 NLT
9. Derr, Jane Ann, *I Don't Like to do Dishes*, Christian Woman, May 1962, Vol. 30, Number 5.
10. Supporting Scriptures: Matt. 20:26-28; 22:36-39; 25:31-40.

The Mercy of God

1. Ps.139:7-12 NLT
2. Rom.11:32 NLT
3. Col.1:15-23 NLT
4. Ps. 8:1-9 NLT
5. Ps 119:73-80 MSG
6. Supporting Scriptures - Poem
   Ex. 17:14; Job 19:23-27; Ps. 136; Hosea 4:1; Joel 3:44; Zech. 14:1-9; Phil. 2:4-8; 3:13-14; 4:13; Col. 3:14; Rev. 1:1-2; 22:3

The Eternal God formed Me

1. Ps. 139:13-16 NLT
2. Spafford, Horatio G. *It is well with my soul…when peace like a river attendeth my way, when sorrows like sea billows roll, whatever my lot, thou has taught me to say, it is well with my soul.* 1873. Music: Phillip P. Bliss 1876.
3. Ps. 90:12 NLT
4. Ps. 62:1-2 NLT
5. 1 Pet. 1:24-25 NLT
6. Ps.1:1-6 ESV
7. Gal. 3:27 ESV
8. Rev. 22:1-2 ESV
9. John 4:13-14 ESV
10. 2 Tim. 3:16 ESV
11. Rom. 13:8-10 ESV
12. Jere. 17:7-10 ESV
13. Goldbaum, Kate, *What is the Oldest Tree in the World?* www.livescience.com/29152-oldest-tree-in-the-world.html 8/27/2017
14. Ps. 139:16 NLT
15. Ps. 56:8 NLT
16. Supporting Scriptures: Matt. 5-6; Matt. 7:7; Matt. 7:18-20; Acts 7:56-58; Ex. 20:1-21; Mark 9:2-12; Mark 13:5-37; Luke 22:14-20; Acts 28:20; Mark 8:2-12; Jude 8-16; 2 Kings 1:18-2 Kings 2:1-15; Heb. 4:1-16; Phil. 4:13; Acts 28:23; Deut. 34; John 20:29; Heb. 4:1-16; Heb. 5:1-6; Rev. 20:12; 21:27; Phil. 4:3.
17. John 20:30-31 NLT

18. Heb. 4:14-16 NLT
19. Isa. 40:6-8 NLT

Response to God's Greatness and Grace

1. Ps. 139: 17-18 NLT
2. Ps. 40:5 NLT
3. Acts 7:1-59 NLT
4. Derr, Jane Ann *God's House! Beautiful! Let's Go*! Asa Frakes Story
5. Fisher, Lee *Fire from the Hills*, Henderson Settlement, the Story of Parson Frakes and the Henderson Settlement. Frakes, Kentucky. Condensed and used by permission from Fire in the Hills by Lee Fisher and the Henderson Settlement 2005.
6. Gibson, Mark, *A Journey of Forgiveness*. Gibson Associate Director of Communication and Marketing at ISTU. Indiana State University Magazine Volume 8, Number 2 Fall 2005. Permission letter given July 7, 2016 by Libby Roerig, Director of Communications, Editor STATE Magazine, Indiana State University, 104 Gillum Hall, Terre Haute, Indiana 47809
7. Single Woman Missionary to Arabic speaking Muslims, Permission letter given but requested name be withheld.
8. Mansoori, Ozden and Kevin, March 2018
9. Sproul, R. C. *God's Holiness*. Google search www.bible.org R.C. Sproul January 20, 2018. Supporting Scriptures listed: 1 Sam. 2:2; Ps. 86:8-10; 99:103; Isa. 40:35; 57:15; 6:3-5; Hab. 1:13a

~Part Four – God's Holiness
Supporting Scriptures: I Sam. 2:2; Ps. 86:8-10; 99:1-3; Is. 6-5; 40:25; 57:15; Hosea 11:13a.

Mysteries and Secrets

1. Ps. 139:19-22 NLT
2. Deut. 29:29 ESV
3. Rev. 12:7-12; Rev. 12:17 NLT
4. Jude 4-10 NLT
5. Ps. 34:7 MSG
6. Dan. 10:1-21 NLT
7. Dan. 12:1-4 NLT
8. Dan.2:19-23 NLT
9. Dan. 2:47 NLT
10. Col. 1:26-27 NLT

11. Eph.1:9 NLT
12. Eph. 6:19-26 NLT
13. Col. 4: 3-4 NLT
14. 1 Tim. 3:16 NLT
15. 1 Cor. 4:1 NLT
16. Col. 2:1-3
17. Rom.16:25-27 NLT
18. Job 1:6-12 MSG
19. Rev.12:9 NLT
20. Gen. 3:1-15 MSG
21. International Standard Bible Encyclopedia, Eerdmans Publishing Co. Grand Rapids, Michigan 1957. Volume IV; Pages 2693 – 2696.
22. Supporting Scriptures: Ezek. 28; Job 1 & 2; Luke 4:6.
23. Ferry, Allen, Dr. Chaplain (Colonel)), sermon at Triad Baptist Church, Kernersville, North Carolina July 9, 2017
24. Isa. 40: 1-31 NLT
25. Col. 1:15-20 NLT
26. 1 Cor. 1:35-58 NLT

The War in our Minds

1. Prov. 11:2 NLT
2. Prov. 9:10 NLT
3. Prov. 1:28-31 NLT
4. Prov. 21:2 NLT1
5. Prov.19:21 NLT
6. Prov. 19:2 NLT
7. 1 Tim. 1:12-17 NLT

My Breath-Taking Experience

1. Ps. 139:23-24 NLT
2. Jeremiah, David, *I never Thought That I'd See the Day*! Chapter 8
3. Derr, Jane Ann *Trailblazing with God Learning to Walk on the Water*. Letters October 13, 1964 and April 3, 1965 Kumasi, Ghana, West Africa
4. Supporting Scripture: Matt. 18:21-35
5. 1 Peter 5:6-11 NLT
6. Milton, Michael A. *Hit by Friendly Fire,*
7. Supporting Scripture: 1 Cor. 10:12 NLT
8. Derr, Jane Ann, *God's House! Beautiful! Let's Go*!
9. Jere. 17:9-10 NLT

10. Matt. 11:28-30 NLT
11. John 17:1-4 NLT
12. Col. 1:15-20 NLT
13. Gal. 6:17 NLT
14. Gal. 2:20-21 NLT
15. Eccl. 5:19-20 & 6:9 NLT
16. Eccl. 7:4 & 20 NLT
17. Eccl. 12:13-14 NLT
18. Isa. 65:17 NLT
19. Matt. 26:36-40 NLT
20. John 17:1-4 NLT
21. Prov. 30:5-6 NLT
22. Isa. 57:15 NLT
23. Isa. 66:2 NLT
24. Prov.11:2 NLT
25. Prov. 22:3 NLT
26. Prov. 29:23 NLT
27. Prov. 28:13 NLT
28. James 4:5-7 NLT
29. Luke 23:34 NLT
30. Rom. 4:7-8 NLT
31. Ps. 32:1-4 NLT
32. Mark 11:25 NLT
33. Eph. 4:32 NLT
34. Col. 3:13 NLT

~Part Five
How to Begin your Journey with Joy
Ps. 139:1-24 (NLT)

Appendix – Charts

No. 1 The Bible is all one Story
Halley, Henry H. *Halley's Bible Handbook,* Zondervan Publishing House, 24th Edition 1965, Page 740

No. 2 Who is God?
Adapted from references from these various sources.
Tozer, A.W. *The Attributes of God, A Journey into the Father's Heart, Volume 1; Deeper Into the Father's Heart, Volume 2;* Wing Spread Publishers; Camp Hill, Pennsylvania; 2001.

Evans, Tony, *The Power of God's Names,* Harvest House Publishers, Eugene, OR; 2014

Lawson, Steven, J. *The Attributes of God, DVD;* Ligonier Ministries, 2015.

No. 3 The Portraits of Jesus in Old Testament Fulfilled in the New Testament.

Adapted from information found in various sources and Beasley, Robert, C. *101 Portraits of Jesus in the Hebrew Scriptures;* Living Stone Books, Hendersonville, NC; 2008.

No. 4 Satan's Work on Earth

Adapted from several sources and

Thompson, Frank Charles, *Thompson Chain Reference Bible NIV;* BB Kirkbride Bible Co., Inc. Page 1569 Satan and Evil Spirits

No. 5 Six Steps to Our Destiny

Adapted from years of study of many courses

No. 6 The Battles of Life

Adapted from several sources and Thompson, Frank Charles, *Thompson Chain Reference Bible,* NIV BB Kirkbride Bible Co., Inc. references on pages 1368 and 1369; Ex.14:13-14; 23.27; 2 Sam. 5:24; 2 Chron. 20:29; Neh. 4:20; Ps. 24:8; Is. 25:25:1 & 9; Zech. 14:3; Phil. 4:10-13; Rev. 7:9, 13-17.

Resources for Further Study

Bonhoeffer, Dietrich, 1906 – 1945. *Life Together. The Classic Exploration of Faith in Community*. Translated and with an introduction by John W. Doberstein. Harper San Francisco. Bonhoeffer was martyred by the Gestapo near the end of World War II for plotting to assassinate Hitler. He left behind a legacy of writings that has become a prized testimony of faith and courage for Christians around the world.

Bounds, E. M. *The Complete Works of E. M. Bounds on Prayer*

Bullinger, E. W. *Word Studies on the Holy Spirit*, A most valuable book for anyone seriously studying key words in the Bible.

Chan, Francis *Forgotten God: Reversing Our Tragic Neglect of the Holy Spirit*.

Chan Francis *Remembering the Forgotten God: An Interactive Workbook for Individual and Small Group Study*

Chand, Samuel R. *Leadership Pain The Classroom for Growth* 2015 Thomas Nelson, Inc. Nashville, TN "God is more willing to use flawed men and women to accomplish his purposes. That's a good thing because none of the other kind is available. Resilient people allow their pain to spur growth instead of collapsing in self-pity." Sam Chand.com

Eareckson, Joni Tada with Steven Estes *When God Weeps – Why Our Sufferings Matter to the Almighty*

Evans, Tony *The Power of God's Names.* 2014 Harvest House Publishers.com

Ferguson, Sinclair, *Who is the Holy Spirit?* 2012. DVD twelve-part-lectures with a great paper study guide. Every lecture presents powerful, dynamic truths that will impact your life now and in the future. Ligonier.org.

Foster, Richard J. *Prayer, Finding the Heart's True Home* 1992 Harper Collins.

Foster, Richard J. *Sanctuary of the Soul, Journey into meditative prayer.* 2011 IVP Books. "We begin this exercise of meditative prayer out of an inner longing, but only as it become a holy habit will we stay with it."

Gibson, Robert Leon Christian, You Were Baptized in Water and the Holy Spirit.

Graham, Billy *The Holy Spirit: Activating God's Power in Your Life*

Hendricks, Howard G. with William D. Hendricks 2007 *Living by the Book, the Art and Science of Reading the Bible.* Moody Publishers, Chicago, Il. The course includes a four-disc DVD plus a book and a workbook. Anyone who seriously wants to study the Bible should get this entire series. It is life-changing. It is a great small group study.

Highfield, Ron *Great Is the Lord. Theology for the Praise of God* 2008 Wm B. Eerdmans Publishing. Eerdmans.com Highfield has developed a great textbook on the Trinity. This reveals a breadth of research unusual in a text of this kind.

Jeremiah, David *Prayer the Great Adventure*

Johnson, Luke Timothy *Early Christianity—The Experience of the Divine.* This twelve lesson DVD course is very insightful and beautifully presented. www.TheGreatCourse.com

Johnson, Luke Timothy. *Jesus and the Gospels* —-thirty-six lesson DVD Series, extremely well-done and presented with great passion. www.TheGreatCourse.com

Keller, W. Phillip *A Gardener Looks at the Fruits of the Spirit.*

Lawrence, Brother *The Practice of the Presence of God* The spiritual secrets of a humble brother who enjoyed closeness with God. A seventeenth–century French monk.

Lightfoot, Neil R. *Everyone's Guide to Hebrews*. 2012 Baker Books.com. If you want to really know who our beautiful Savior is, you would enjoy this book. It has questions at the end of each chapter. This book makes a great small group study guide.

Lightfoot, Neil R. *How We Got the Bible*, Third Edition revised and expanded 2007 Baker Books.com. This book is the fortieth anniversary edition. This is a well-researched book that uncovers facts of history's most fascinating archaeological discoveries including the Sinaitic Manuscripts, the Oxyrhynchus Papyri and the Dead Sea Scrolls. It is concise and engaging.

Lyons, David and Linda Lyons Richardson. *Don't Waste the Pain Learning to grow through suffering.* 2010 NavPress.com Journals of a woman going through cancer. Linda's brother David helped to put the journals together. This is well written with pain and joy balanced. Her last words: "Where will your pain lead you?"

Murray, Andrew *Experiencing the Holy Spirit*

Packer, J. I. *Knowing God*, J. 1973. Excellent book with Scripture.

Parrish, Archie, *A Simple Way to Pray – The Wisdom of Martin Luther on Prayer.*

Powell, Mark E. *Centered in God. The Trinity and Christian Spirituality 2014* Abilene Christian University Press. Powell takes a difficult concept and puts it into easy to comprehend thoughts. A valuable book to give the Christian a vision of God.

Ryrie, Charles *The Holy Spirit.*

Sproul, R. C. *The Holiness of God*, Excellent book plus a Study Guide Book

Sproul, R. C. *Knowing Scripture* 2009 IVP Books, Downers Grove Il This is a very practical, easy to read tool

Sproul, R. C. *Surprised By Suffering* 2010 The role of pain and death in the Christian life. Reformation Trust Publishing. A division of Ligonier Ministries.

Stanley, Charles F. *Courageous Faith. My story from a life of obedience.* 2016 Howard Books. One of Stanley's best books.

Stanley, Charles F. *Living in the Power of the Holy Spirit*

Stott, John *Baptism and Fullness: The Work of the Holy Spirit Today*

Strobel, Lee, *The Case for Christ* A Journalistic Personal Investigation of the Evidence for Jesus 1998 Zondervan.com. A fascinating treatment of this subject. Every inquirer should have this book.

Strobel, Lee, *The Case for Grace. A Journalist Explores the Evidenced of Transformed Lives.* 2015 A great book with study guides. Zondervan.com

Tozer, A.W. 1897-1963 *The Attributes of God* –Part 1 A Journey into the Heart of God *The Attributes of God*—Part 2 Deeper into the Father's Heart Excellent books with study guides

Wald, Oletta, *The Joy of Discovery in Bible Study* 2002 Augsburg Fortress Minneapolis This book discusses how to make Bible charts to focus on chapter and book themes.

Willard, Dallas Albert 1935-2013 *The Allure of Gentleness. Defending the Faith in the manner of Jesus 2015* Harper Collins. This is a must read for anyone who is trying to lead people to Christ. This was published and organized by Dallas Willard's daughter Rebecca Willard Heatley in June 2014. She transcribed his talks from a four-part series. They were working on this book together when he developed cancer and died. He prayed, "May this book help us to be simple, humble, and thoughtful as we listen to others and help them come to faith in the One who has given us life."

Yancey, Philip *Prayer – Does it Make a Difference?* 2006 Zondervan. A very powerful book on prayer written with much research but in an easy way to follow each new concept.

Yancey, Philip *What is So Amazing about Grace? And Where is God When it Hurts? 2008*

Appendix 1
CHARTS

CHART #1

THE BIBLE IS ALL ONE STORY				
KEY CONCEPT	**GENESIS**	**REVELATION**	**OUTCOME**	**WHAT REMAINS?**
Heaven & Earth	Old removed 1:1	Made new 21:1	New remains	New Heaven & New Earth
Sea	Called together 1:10	No more 21:1	No more	
Night	Night 1:5	No night 21:25	No more	
Sun & Moon	Sun & Moon 1:16	No more 21:23	No more	
Death	Death 2:17	No more 21:4	No more	
Pain	Multiply pain 3:16	No more 21:4	No more	
Curse	Curse 3:17	No more 22:3	No more	
Satan	Satan 3:1 & 4	No more 20:10	No more	
Tree of Life	Taken away 3:22-24	Re-appears 22:2	Re-appears	Tree of Life
God's Presence	Disappears 3:24	Re-appears 22:4	Re-appears	God's Presence
River Home	Home taken 2:10	Re-appears 22:1		

WHAT REMAINS?

New Heaven and New Earth

The Tree of Life

God's Presence — the Father, Son, and Holy Spirit

Our Home by the River

Who would not want to read this Beautiful Story?

CHART #2

WHO IS GOD?	
SUBJECT	**SCRIPTURE**
ETERNALNESS	Is. 57:15; Ps. 90:1-2
FAITHFULNESS	Gen. 8:20-22; 9:8-16; Ps. 89:1-2,5,8,24; 105:8; Is. 54:2-9; Matt 5:18; 11:28; Luke 15:12; John 11:24; 1 Tim 2:13; 2 Tim 2:13; 1 Thess. 8:24; 1 John 1:7 & 9; 2:1; 4:16
GOD IS NOT IN TIME	Heb 13:8; Ps. 90:12; John 8:58; John 14:28; John 10:30; Matt 5:21-22; Heb. 2:15; Rev. 13:8
GOODNESS	Is. 63:7-9; Deut. 30:9; Ps. 34:8 & 31; Matt. 7:11; Ps. 36:7; 119:68; 139:17
GRACE	Gen. 6:8; Prov. 3:34; Rom. 3:24; Eph. 1:6-7; Ex. 33:17; John 1:16-17; Rom. 5:15; 1 Peter 5:10; Rev. 13:8; John 14:6; Acts 4:12; Ez. 37:3; 1 Peter 1:10-12; 1 Tim. 3:16; Luke 15:11-17; 1 John 1:9
HOLINESS	Ex. 15:11; Job 25:5-6; Prov. 9:10; Ex. 19:9-14; Job 15:15; Ps. 22:3; Is. 6:3; Prov. 9:10; 30:3; Ex. 13:21-22; 2 Peter 3:7,10-12; Hab. 1:12-13; Lam. 3:22; Prov. 9:10; 1 Peter 1:16; Is. 33:14; Act 13:2; Heb. 12:29; Rev. 1:17; 7:11-15
IMMANENCE	Ps. 139: 8-10; Is. 40:12,15, 26; 1 Kings 8:27; Acts 17:27-28; Rom. 8:15; Col. 3:3; 10; Gal. 4:6; 2 Peter 1:4;
IMMUTABILITY	Ps. 139:8-10; Mal 3:6; Matt. 28:20; John 14:9; Heb. 6:17-18; 13:8; 1 Tim. 1:15; James 1:17
JUSTICE	Gen. 18:25; Deut. 10:17; Ps. 19:9; 92:15; 97:2; Is. 28:17; Eze. 18:20; Rev. 16:5-7
LOVE	Ps. 9:4; 41:3; 104:31; Zep. 3:7; Luke 2:14; 15:20; 16:22-23; John 20:16; Rom. 5:8; 1 Cor. 13:12; 2 Cor. 5:17; Heb. 2:6; 7:25; 1 John 4:7-21,18
MERCY	Ps. 103:8-17; Ex. 34:4-7; 2 Chron. 5:13-14; Is. 63:7-9; Ez. 33:11; 37-3; Ex. 2:23-25; Mark 9:31; Is. 6:2; Mark 6:34-37; Ps. 103:13; Ps. 136; Lam. 3:22; 2 Peter 3:9; Rom. 2:4; Matt. 16:22; Rev. 5:12
OMNIPOTENT	Gen. 17:1; Ex. 3:14; Job 38:11; Ps. 41:3; 62:11; Matt. 11:16-17; 19:26; Luke 1:37; 11:2; John 17:3; Rom. 1:20; Eph. 1:16; 2 Pet 1:24; Rev 19:6

WHO IS GOD?	
SUBJECT	**SCRIPTURE**
OMNIPRESENCE	Gen. 18:21; 32:22-32 1 Kings 8:27; Acts 17:27-28; Ps. 139:1-12; Luke 5:8; 1 John 3:2; 2 Peter 1:4; Gal. 4:6; Ps. 16:8; Ps. 32; Jer. 23;23-24; Matt. 28:20; Eph. 2:1-3; 4:17-19; 2 Chron. 2:6; Eph. 2:12; Rom. 8:15;
OMNISCIENCE	Heb 4:13; 1 Cor. 2:7-11; Titus 1:2; Mal 3:6; Luke 1:37; 2 Tim 2:13; Matt 11:25-27; 1 Cor.. 2:1-5; Rom 11:33-36; John 2:24-25; 1 Tim 3:16; Mark 7:37; Luke 15:2
SELF EXISTENCE	Gen. 1:1; Ex. 3:11-15; Mal. 4:2; Job 1:8; Rom. 1:26; Eph. 2:2
SOVEREIGNTY	Deut. 4:39; 32:39-40; Job 12:9-17; 33:13; Jer. 18:6: Dan. 4:3 & 35: Nah. 1:2; Col 1:16-17
SOVEREIGNTY/ FREE WILL	Gen. 1:1; Josh. 24:15; Job 33:13; Luke 16:22-23; 24:13-32; Acts 1:25; Rev. 4:1 3; 5:9
TRANSCENDENCE	1 Chron. 39:11; Ps. 145:3; 1 Tim 6:16; Is 6:2-3; I Chron. 29:11; Gen. 18:27; Dan 10:15,17; Job 26:14; Is. 55:8-9; Job 26:14; Rev. 4:80; Gen. 28:17; 2 Cor. 12:10
TRINITY	Mark 1:9-11; Luke 3:21-22; John 1:32-34; 1 John 4:12-15
WISDOM	Prov. 3:19; Jer. 10:12; Rom. 16:27; Job 12:13; Eph. 1:8; 3:10; Gen. 1:26; 2:19; I Thess. 4:16-17; Rev. 4:11; 5:9-12

CHART #3

Portraits of Jesus In OT Fulfilled in NT			
Text	**Theme**	**Explanation**	**Importance**
Genesis 1.1	Creation	Existed in the beginning	Christ is God
John 1: 1-3	Creator	All created through him	Part of Trinity
Genesis 2:7 & 23	Humanity created	Bone and Flesh	In image of God
Genesis 3	Satan & Evil	Flesh and Blood	New life force
Revelation 12.7	War in Heaven	Satan cast to earth	War now on earth
Genesis 3:14	Satan crushed	Christ will bruise him	Blood life force
Genesis 3:21	Blood cover	God clothed Adam/Eve	Blood first named
Genesis 9:4	Life in blood	Blood atonement	Power of blood
Romans 5:12	Cosmic treason	Evil/shedding of blood	Christ redemption

CHART #4

SATAN'S WORK ON EARTH		
Old Testament	**New Testament**	**Satan Activities**
Job 1:12		God permits him to test Job
Gen. 4-5 1 Chron. 21:1		Tempts the disobedient
Job 1:9-11		Slanders the saints
Job 2:7		Inflicts diseases
Zech. 3:1		Opposes the righteous
	Luke 4:6	Claims authority over world
	Acts 26:18	Sinners are under his dominion
	2 Cor. 4:3-4	Blinds eyes of unbelievers
	Eph. 6:12	Contends with saints
	2 Thess. 2:9; Heb. 2:14	Inspires counterfeit miracles
	Matt. 4:1-3	Tempts Christ
	Matt. 13:19	Removes the good seed
	Matt. 13:38-39	Sows the weeds
	Luke 9:42; 13:16	Ruins soul and body
	John 8:44	Satan lies
	John 13:2; Acts 5:2 2 Cor. 12:7; Eph. 2:2	Instigates people to sin
	1 Peter 5:8; Rev. 2:10	Preys on people
	Matt. 4:6	Misuses Bible Passages

CHART #5

STAIR-STEPS TO OUR DESTINY

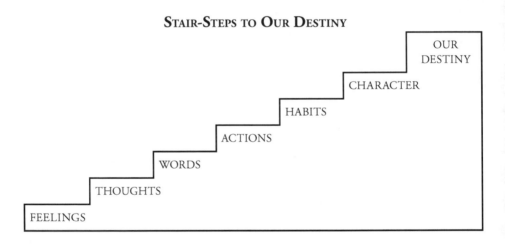

Chart #6

BATTLE OF LIFE		
Bible Verse	**Armor or Weapons**	**The Victory or Outcome**
Ex. 14:13-14	Keep silent Remain calm	God will fight for you
Ex. 23:27	God will send terror & confusion	Enemies will turn back & run
2 Sam. 5:24	Wait, Listen then move quickly	God went out in front & struck enemies
2 Chron. 20:29	Fear of the Lord God	God fought against the enemy
Neh. 4:20	Listen	Divine guidance
Ps. 24:8	Trust in God	Divine guidance
Zech. 14:3	Trust in God	Conquered enemy
Phil. 4:10-13	Strength through Christ	Contentment
Is. 25:1 & 9	Praise God & wait	Christ came after they waited
Rev. 7:9 & 13-17	Washed robes	Salvation Given Shelter
	Blood of Christ	food and water
	Died for Christ	God wipes away tears
		Stands in front of God's
		Throne then serves God

Appendix 2
PHOTO GALLERY

Roots

Prairie Creek, Indiana 1914. Jane Ann's mother, Luetta Collins, her older sister Esther, her younger sister Leota, their parents Robert L. Collins and mother, Autensia Jewell Collins. Esther is sitting in the front seat with her Daddy. This car was a 1914 Model T Touring car. Henry Ford's first version built on his first moving assemble line.

Terre Haute, Indiana 1937, the Loran Critchlow Family. Back row:
Loran; Jane Ann's Dad, middle row; Loran's little sister Ruby. Luetta,
Jane Ann's mother is holding Jack and Ruby is holding Jane Ann.

San Diego, California, in 1970's; Loran and Luetta Critchlow, Jane Ann's parents.

Terre Haute, Indiana, 1959. Harold's parents, Tonie and Susie Derr

Terre Haute, Indiana. Northside Church of Christ. December 24, 1950. Harold came home from Keesler Air Force Base in Biloxi, Mississippi for the wedding. Jane Ann made her wedding dress and carried her new white Bible with her under the bouquet of flowers.

Georgia House Memories November 1993 to October 2014

Cumming, Georgia, 2011. The completed, restored home with over three acres in the woods. Harold and Jane Ann bought this house in 1992. Harold fervently worked every month to add beauty and additional rooms for their large family gatherings. The adults enjoyed gathering on the porch, swinging, listening to the water fall from the fountain, and talking, while the grandchildren and great-grandchildren were outside exploring nature and playing games.

2004, Harold, John and Libby the Labrador puppy that John gave his Dad. They are in front of the beautiful fountain that John built for Jane Ann for Mother's Day. All the family enjoyed John's lovely gift.

John F. Kennedy International Airport, Jamaica, New York, 1991. John Derr inside of a TWA plane, where he worked as an Inflight Service Manager. He was awarded a Certificate of Achievement from the Department of the Army in recognition of his personal contribution to operation "DESERT SHIELD" and "DESERT STORM" for his personal commitment and professionalism while on duty in a hostile environment.

Cumming, Georgia, 2011. This is the sunroom where Jane Ann sat reflecting on how to begin this book. The round oak table, the place where Harold died, family reunions held, the antique grand piano that John refurbished for her, where Bible classes were held, the woods, the voices of past parties, weddings, tears and laughter, and where the unexpected flood happened. This sunroom was a great gift from God to the entire Derr family and a special place for their healing after Harold's death.

Cumming, Georgia late 1990's. Harold had the privilege of performing the marriage ceremony for their granddaughter, Shauna and her husband Jeremy Lacow. Later they celebrated with a party in the sunroom for both families of sixty people. This picture only includes their adult children and Deborah and Cathy's husbands.

Cumming, Georgia late 1990's. This picture includes the entire Derr family in their living room, their grandchildren and their husbands who attended Shauna's wedding.

Sawnee Center, Cumming, Georgia July 2000. Harold and Jane Ann at the celebration of their fiftieth wedding anniversary. They were immersed in a joyous week-end celebration event for their entire family.

Sawnee Center, Cumming, Georgia July 2000. Family came from great distances for the special event. Family from Indiana: Harold's brother Gene and his wife Rosemary; their daughter and her family Denise and Carl Malm and their two sons, Eric and Kyle and Jane Ann's brother Jack Critchlow and his wife Betty. Family from North Carolina: Their daughter Deborah and her husband Kevin McLaughlin, with their daughter Tara and her husband Shane Inman. Family from Georgia: Their daughter, Diana Eddins and her daughters, Amanda and Katherine and married daughter Shauna and her husband Jeremy Lacow. Family from Boise, Idaho: their. daughter Janice Becker and her children, Elaine, Luke, Claire, and Adria. Family from Tennessee: Cathy and her husband Roger Lagotte and their two daughters Helene and Rachelle. Family from New York: their son John and longtime family friends from Washington State: Paula Campbell with her mother and aunt Helen.

Cumming, Georgia 2004, in the front yard of their home. Harold
and Jane Ann with their five children. Left to right, Janice, Deborah,
Harold, Jane Ann, Diana, John and Cathy. Family came to celebrate the
marriage of Janice to Tim White. Harold performed the ceremony in
the back yard in front of the special arbor he made for the wedding.

Cumming, Georgia, 2004. In the front yard of the Derr home.
Harold and Jane Ann with most of their extended family.

We trust, travel and transition together
Trust

Amanda Gallegos, the Derr's granddaughter in front of the tomb of her twins Bram and Kopeland. After being airlifted to Dallas, Texas from Las Cruses, New Mexico, November 30, 2009 Amanda gave birth to co-joined twins. The twins lived until December 30, 2009. Amanda, Joseph and their older son, Ethan, grieved as well as the entire family Each year after this, on the twin's birthday, the entire family celebrates by each releasing helium balloons to the twins until the time they will be reunited again.

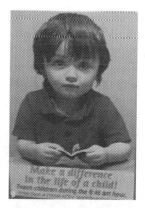

May 17. 2015. Oak Hills Church, San Antonio, Texas. This is Avery Gallegos, who is the poster child for the Children's Ministry at the church where Max Lacado, is the lead pastor. Avery is a great gift to Amanda and Joseph after losing the twins. Amanda and Joseph now,live in Hawaii where Joseph is stationed in the Army. Now they also have a beautiful daughter Gracelynn who is nearly two. God is gracious, and God is good.

Travel

May 2011, Imperial Jewels of China Viking River Cruise. Cathy celebrating completing her MBA degree by taking her sister, Janice on a trip to China. Cathy and Janice on board for their flight from Minneapolis to Tokyo. They are so ready to start their most excellent adventure.

Cathy and Janice standing on the Great Wall of China. The Great Wall was generally built to protect the Chinese states and empires against the raids and invasions of the various nomadic groups of the Eurasian Steppe. Most of the existing wall is from the Ming Dynasty (1368 – 1644). The wall once stretched for more than 6,200 miles.

Kernersville, North Carolina 2012. Diana and Jane Ann took a 2,600-mile trip to New England in October 2012. On the first stop of this trip, they visited Deborah and Kevin McLaughlin. This is Deborah and Kevin with Diana in front of the McLaughlin home.

Washington, DC mid-October 2012. Diana and Jane Ann in front of a statue in the heart of Washington, DC. Parking was difficult. Walks were long. They decided to only visit the Smithsonian, then head to New York to visit John.

Forest Hills, New York, October 2012. John, Ellen McMahon and Jane
Ann. Diana and Jane Ann were able to visit John for a couple of days. He
worked as a real estate broker in Forest Hills and Ellen had been his co-
worker for many years. John and Ellen gave us a sightseeing tour of Forest
Hills, and John's friend Jim Villa gave us a sightseeing tour of Manhattan.

Sunderland, Massachusetts, October 13, 2012. Stephen Broyles and Jane Ann in front of a Buttonball Tree. This tree is believed to be the largest tree of its kind on the East Coast. It is believed to be seeded before 1665. Stephen was the editor of Jane Ann's second book. Although Jane Ann lived in Georgia and Stephen lived in Massachusetts, they were able to accomplish this work entirely through emails. Stephen invited Diana and Jane Ann to visit him on their New England trip and to let him be their sightseeing guide. After seeing the beautiful colorful leaves at the peak of God's glory, they saw the Emily Dickinson Museum and the Library Building at the University of Massachusetts. This twenty-eight -story building was completed in 1973. Within two months of opening, brick chips began to fall from the side of the tower. According to one version of the rumor, the weight of the books was heavier than expected and as a result, the library was subsiding slowly into the earth. A different rumor maintains that the building was built on pond-saturated grounds leading to sinking. After the good-byes, Diana and Jane Ann were on to their next stop, Newport, Rhode Island to visit the historic Vanderbilt Marble House and other historic mansions. Diana and Jane Ann had a great trip in every way. However, they were stunned a few days later, on October 29, to learn the area that they had explored only days before, had experienced Superstorm Sandy and this devasting storm caused widespread extensive damage.

Transition

Cumming, Georgia sunroom, 2013. John and his puppy, Samantha came to visit Jane Ann after the flood. "Mom! What were you thinking? I think you need to downsize and move near Deborah and Kevin in North Carolina."

Cumming, Georgia 2013 Jack Critchlow, Jane Ann's brother from Indiana and Jane Ann in front of the fireplace. Although miles had always separated them, they tried to stay in touch. Jack came to visit and to tell the Georgia house good-bye before Jane Ann moved to North Carolina.

Cumming, Georgia 2014 Cathy and her husband Mark Ellis taking a few moments to laugh while working with all the family trying to downsize their mother's home to prepare for the move to North Carolina.

Kernersville, North Carolina 2015, Janice and Jane Ann love to spend hours talking. Janice took time off work in 2006 to help Jane Ann go through hospice care of Harold. Later Janice spent many years as a hospice care volunteer in Colorado. Tim was also a hospice volunteer who once took a long-stemmed rose to a dying 96-year-old woman with no family.

Kernersville, North Carolina 2015. Cathy and Jane Ann reflecting on the move from Georgia to North Carolina. They smile as they reflect how great it is for her to be able to have a smaller, more manageable, organized home and the blessing of being near to Deborah. They laughed at all the blunders, struggles, and pitfalls that God had covered by His Amazing Grace.

Kernersville, North Carolina 2016. Tim and Janice from Littleton, Colorado visiting Jane Ann and sharing stories about the move and her new life. Tim smiles because he no longer needs to do twenty repair jobs for his visit, instead he can just sightsee, talk and enjoy the moment.

Kernersville, North Carolina 2016. Kevin and Tim standing proudly behind the beautiful kitchen island cart they had just put together as a gift for Jane Ann. Yes, she is blessed beyond words.

Kernersville, North Carolina, 2017. Jane Ann's living room. Cathy and Mark Ellis came to visit from Brentwood, Tennessee. Kevin, Deborah, Cathy and Mark. This picture was taken after Kevin had taken them to a nearby restaurant. They always get a take-home dessert to eat around the round oak table and share their stories in this present, precious time together

We experience New Hope and New Joy together
Hope

Kernersville, North Carolina, 2017 Triad Baptist Church, Deborah and Jane Ann celebrating Mother

Joy

Kernersville, North Carolina, January 2019. Kevin was diagnosed with cancer in 2018, Deborah, Kevin and Jane Ann celebrating Kevin's completion of the cancer treatments.

Kernersville, North Carolina, January 2019. Deborah, Kevin and Diana sitting around the round oak table. Diana came all the way from her home in Honolulu to celebrate Kevin's birthday. After nearly a year and a half of cancer treatments consisting of chemo and radiation, they were all elated to have this priceless celebration together. Praise God for His unfailing love, mercy, grace and kindness!

Kernersville, North Carolina, Ladies in Discovery Bible Class, January 2019. Jane Ann with her daughter Diana. The class had a surprise Birthday party for Jane Ann, presented her flowers and gifts. The food was delicious, and the time together was precious. Since Diana was in town from Honolulu, she was able to attend the party

Kernersville, North Carolina, May 2019. Deborah and Jane Ann celebrating the completion of this book. Deborah spent many hours editing carefully all the book. It could not have been completed without her excellent help. Praise God for her effort and many prayers toward this end.

Jane Ann Derr's Prior Books

Trailblazing with God is author Jane Ann Derr's account of how she and her husband Harold with their five children went to Ghana, West Africa, in the early 1960's a time of political upheaval in Africa as well as America.

Xulon Press 2008
ISBN 978-1-60477-866-3
Order from the author at www.christianreading.com/jderr or writerjanederr@gmail.com
Also online at Amazon.com and available for download on most eReader platforms.

"In *God's House! Beautiful! Let's Go!* Jane Ann Derr has told us more than we have a right to ask. She has let us into the world of her marriage, her family, her work, her loss, her fears, and her happiness. She has let us into her faith in God and her devotion to Jesus Christ. She has let us into her husband's illness and death, and into the grief and resolve of her life as the one who survived. But her real interest is what she has seen of the goodness and mercy of God."

Stephen E. Broyles, author of *The Wind that Destroys and Heals*

God's House! Beautiful! Let's Go!
Xulon Press 2011
ISBN 978 1612 1579 93
Order from the author at <u>writerjanederr@gmail.com</u> or
<u>www.christianreading.com/jderr</u>
Also is available online at Amazon.com and
Is available for download on most e-reader platforms.

Printed in the United States
By Bookmasters